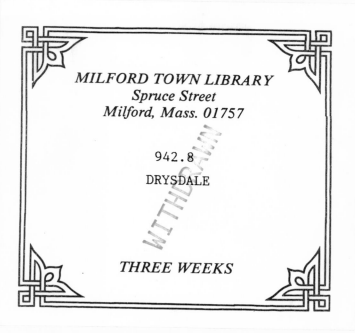

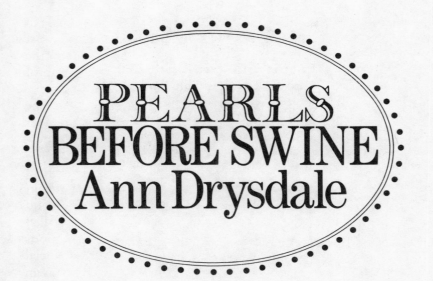

PEARLS BEFORE SWINE
Ann Drysdale

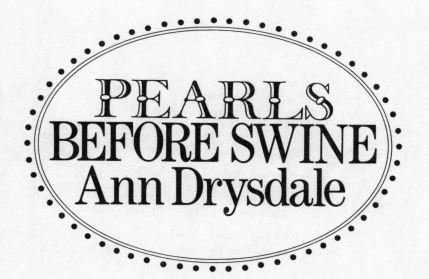

PEARLS BEFORE SWINE
Ann Drysdale

Routledge & Kegan Paul
London, Boston, Melbourne and Henley

First published in 1985
by Routledge & Kegan Paul plc

14 Leicester Square, London WC2H 7PH, England

9 Park Street, Boston, Mass. 02108, USA

464 St Kilda Road, Melbourne,
Victoria 3004, Australia and

Broadway House, Newtown Road,
Henley on Thames, Oxon RG9 1EN, England

Set in 11 on 13pt Garamond
by Inforum Ltd
and printed in Great Britain
by Billing and Sons Ltd
Worcester

© Ann Drysdale 1985

Library of Congress Cataloging in Publication Data

Drysdale, Ann.
Pearls before swine.
1. Farm life—England—North Yorkshire.   2. Drysdale
Ann.   3. North Yorkshire—Social life and customs.
I. Title.
S522.G7D792   1985   942.8'10858'0924   85–2397

ISBN 0–7102–0466–3

For David

'By our first strange and fatal interview,
By all desires which thereof did ensue'

Contents

Acknowledgments

The author wishes to thank Mr Robert Graves for his permission to quote from his magical poem 'Allie', and Mr Michael Butler Yeats and Macmillan (London) Ltd for their permission to use part of W.B. Yeats' 'Two Songs of a Fool', and to quote from his diary.

Messrs Charles Kingsley, William Cowper, Gaius Valerius Catullus and John Donne, also quoted, are no longer protected by copyright, but are not, one hopes, beyond reach of the author's gratitude. Thank you, gentlemen.

A Green and Yellow Melancholy

Once upon a time, a prince, lost in a deep, dark forest, came to a clearing where the sun shone down between the blue-black pines onto a mighty rock, from the very centre of which there flowed a tiny, crystal stream. The prince was very thirsty, so he dismounted and knelt to drink a little of the icy water – but to his amazement, it was not water at all, but the sweetest, sparkling wine, and he was struck dumb with surprise. . . .

As I grew up, I began to appreciate the wisdom of his somewhat conservative attitude. In his position I would have run to the stream, fully expecting it to be wine. And it would have been water. I was becoming aware, you see, that I had an unfortunate tendency to expect miracles which I knew to be impossibilities from the outset, and I spent much of my adolescence in a state of wistful disappointment that I have since come to regard as par for the course.

But with the acceptance of the latter attitude as one of my life's constants came a conviction that, even if it were not the more comfortable approach to things, it nevertheless had much to recommend it. True, it obviated the chance of delightful surprises which must momentarily have enriched the life of the wandering prince, but it replaced the element of random gratification with a permanent state of hope, a fierce belief, in defiance of all reason, that becomes in time a very real comfort for its own sake. The gentle melancholy that accompanies it is a rare and peculiarly constructive frame of mind that is surely preferable to a bland acceptance of life at face value, and it still admits of the occasional explosion of joy which fully justifies all that mystic reaching for nothing-in-particular.

My father, tongue-in-cheek, always referred to it as 'The Celtic Twilight'. It has a host of different faces, ranging from the vague and exquisite sadness, the soft fingertip-touch of melancholy that gives poignancy to small and simple things and adds dimensions of awareness, one at a time, like layers of polish on an old and favourite boot, to the huge and un-wieldy grief that breaks like surf on shingle, catching at the ankles. Poor prince, he didn't know what he was missing.

Part of the predisposition to this lifelong condition is the tendency to daydream in childhood which, if unchecked, leads in later years to the weaving and believing of compli-cated fantasies mostly involving the participation of some-one else, which dooms them from the outset.

In my early teens, when the fashion was for young girls to declare their allegiance to popular singers by emblazoning their names across the front of their bodies – Tommy – Elvis – Cliff – the only voice that could rouse me to the peak of pleasure suggested by the squeals and vapours of my con-temporaries was that of the German baritone, Dietrich Fischer-Dieskau, though there was no way such a name could be fitted on the front of one so ill-endowed with bosom.

I listened on radio to his lieder recitals, cut his picture from gramophone catalogues and fell asleep dreaming of his caressing voice singing for me a Schumann song-

> 'Thou'rt like a flower; so winsome
> So pure and fair thou art.
> I look at thee and sadness
> Steals into my heart. . . .'

2

And it was a dream that lasted until I tried to turn it into reality.

Working at the London offices of Ready Mixed Concrete, I operated the switchboard during the lunch hour. I began an innocent flirtation with a middle-aged accountant with a pleasant voice, who took a most flattering interest in me. We met. He played the flute and the piano, and sang in a not untutored baritone whose range he was eager to display to me, along with other accomplishments which he would describe in some detail over glasses of gin after work. This was my first tentative step on the road to ruin, so perhaps in retrospect it was not such a tragedy that I fell flat on my face.

I confided my fantasies, but not my inexperience. And agreed to his suggestion of a day's sick-leave, to be spent in his house in Barnet while his wife was at work. And he sat at the piano; I sat at his feet as he prepared to play – 'a little Schumann,' he said, with a smile.

His hands crashed down on the keyboard and his voice rang out, loud and melodious – in a most spirited rendering of 'The Two Grenadiers'! And for a moment I thought my heart might break.

But it didn't. And the element of self-generated farce has delighted me ever since. Before he had reached the end of the verse, I had begun to laugh, and with all the artless cruelty of the young, I let go of the bruised dream and reached for another. It was much later when I began to wonder whether I had been acting a part in the accountant's dream, perhaps even stepping on it in extricating myself from the ruins of my own. All our growing up is done, to a greater or lesser degree, at the expense of others. How salutary to remember, when it is our turn at the piano!

Dreams are a responsibility, to whomsoever they belong. I remember my first banana, after the austerity of the war. I was given the unprepossessing object, about which I had heard so much, and the thing I most remember, apart from not liking the taste and being slightly disgusted by the texture, is the intensity with which my reaction was observed. I remember my mother's mouth opening with mine, shutting a little before it, encouraging me to chew as it masticated some phantom fruit of its own, miming what was expected of me. I have noticed since how often women feeding toddlers produce this pantomime. I have never seen a man do it. Would I have enjoyed that banana, I wonder, if I had been allowed to practise with it in private?

Caviar, though, was a different story. I tasted it for the first time only a few weeks ago, and the second-hand impressions I had been offered throughout my life had all been depressingly negative. I did not expect to like it.

But I cannot remember when I last tasted anything so delightful. Each little egg perfect and shiny, like the bugle-beads on Granny Davenham's evening bag, escaping over the buttered toast like teeny-weeny eyeballs. Splitting seventeen-at-a-time between the teeth with a splatter of salty juice or giving way with exquisite suddenness, one by one, between tongue and palate. . . .

Perhaps this is a book about dreams.

I have already written a great deal about living in this high and far-off place; about why we came and why we stayed. Part of me was striving to make a place for us in a society whose constant change I could not see; part was trying to recreate the sweet safety of a nursery-rhyme, the predictability of a fairy-tale. It was my dream, and I was ready to take the bananas with the caviar, and to present both with the honesty incumbent upon the presenter of a first-person narrative.

It would be more comfortable, perhaps, to concentrate on the caviar, to recreate only the air of circus that so often surrounds us, to catalogue only the fantasy and the fun. But the result would be insufferably jolly, and something of a waste of the bananas.

I suppose in a way I am apologising for interrupting the

gaiety with the occasional sadness, the tempering of the triumphs with the occasional hurt. But at times I am worried, cold or hungry, and now and then monumentally weary. At times I am puzzled and unhappy, questioning my choice of lifestyle which has enforced upon me a loneliness of spirit that is sometimes hard to bear. Sometimes the conviction that I am triumphantly alone at the helm of a tight ship is superseded by a longing to share, not the life itself, but the needs that brought me to it.

W.B. Yeats wrote in his diary:

Today the thought came to me that —— never really understands my plans, or nature or ideas. Then came the thought – what matter? How much of the best I have done and still do is but the attempt to explain myself to her? If she understood I should lack a reason for writing, and one can never have too many reasons for doing what is so laborious.

Pig Ignorance

It began with Ernest, the gift-pig who came into our lives just as it was all starting to unfold. To him belongs the special aura of firstness that sets apart the people and things with whom and which we begin all our most exciting enterprises – first treasures, first lovers.

To him is owed the joy of discovering that little pigs are hard and firm, their skin downy and dry. From him we learned the basic rules of human behaviour in relation to swine, and through him we set foot on the road to discovery of the place of the pig in the life of the peasant.

When Ernest left us, he left a small, round hurt in the centre of things, like a cigarette-burn in a table-cloth, and the first sow, Rosalie, was brought into our lives to patch it. Not so much the addition of another string to our commercial bow as the bringing-to-life of the Irish halfpenny that was always, with the stuffed fox-head and the small stone bear, counted among my earliest treasures.

It soon became apparent, though, that Rosalie made excellent sense in business terms. Her first few litters made a handsome profit and I congratulated myself on my cleverness. I'm sure that a modern, commercial sow would have been more prolific than our old Rosalie, but I wanted a Gloucester Old Spot, an old-fashioned cottagers' pig, and her robust constitution and pleasant, easy-going nature justified my choice.

For a long time I'd thought we ought to keep a gilt from one of her litters. When I reared Biddy and John, the two tiny pigs from one spring litter, I fully intended to keep Biddy for that purpose, but as she grew, she became ill-tempered and downright mean, snappy with her fellow-creatures and possessive with her food. Her ears stood up belligerently and her snout was long and thin, giving her an overall air of bitchyness that I found distasteful. I was told by all and sundry that she was 'a fine lengthy pig,' but somehow I just didn't like her, so I sold her to someone who did.

The next litter, on the other hand, were different altogether. Snub-nosed, lop-eared, jolly and outgoing like their dam. The only trouble was that there were only two gilts in the litter, so I spent days making my choice. Not the longer pig, the bigger or the better pig – but the nicer pig. And I chose her. Nancy asked what we were going to call her, and I said 'Portia'. It somehow had to do with pigs and with choosing. I went out with a can of gentian violet aerosol and sprayed a huge purple daisy on her bum. 'And here choose I,' I told the assembled pigs. 'Joy be the consequence.'

And so for a while, it proved to be.

Rosalie became a grandmother. She had long since become one of the family. I suppose it must prove something, this immediate affinity of the Drysdales with creatures so universally regarded as lacking in dignity and decency, but nothing, I dare swear, that most people didn't know already.

On that very first morning, when she stepped happily out of her sty, she treated her new home to the benign smile that has since proved not only part of her appearance but also of her personality; from the very first she was Our Pig. Playing cricket with Robert and happily taking on the rotten job – deep field in the nettle patch – or running at full pig-power down the hill with Nancy to their mutual delight; digging in the potato patch for any that have been left behind or just coming to sit beside me while I drink my cup of tea on the front step, she is still the very essence, the summing-up of my highest ideals of piggery.

Portia, however, was something of a disappointment. She grew huge; sailing over the terrain like the Hindenberg. Her face lengthened, her mother's perpetual grin being super-seded by her father's questing weasel-snout. Her Large White ancestry had stamped itself heavily upon her, and I found it almost impossible to satisfy the appetite that went with it. Her first litter left a small profit, but her second consisted of only three pigs. Had she had no pigs at all, I could have looked on it as a personal tragedy for poor Portia, but as things stood I could see it only as a financial disaster. I had begun to see the smallholding no longer as an end in itself, but as a source of income, and from this viewpoint I was forced to examine the relationship between what went in and what came out. In Portia's case, the latter in no way justified the former. Knowledgeable visitors nodded approvingly at her, calling her a fine lengthy pig – a 'really good sort' – but she was, from our point of view, a sad mistake.

I took her three pigs and gave them to Rosalie, who knew perfectly well that they were not hers, but fed and mothered them without argument. And I borrowed a boar, mated her again, and resolved to sell her 'in-pig'. It is only in retrospect that I can appreciate how much of a businesswoman I had become, and I recall with sad amusement how I basked in the approval of the other farmers – 'Now you're *thinking*, missus'. Little did they appreciate just how hard I was trying not to.

Ever since my Mum moved up to Yorkshire, she's been ferreting her way through a huge collection of cardboard boxes containing a lifetime's accumulation of Lord-knows-what so that she can sort the wheat from the chaff, as it were, and dispose of that which is surplus to requirements. Only the huge mountains of similar impedimenta behind the cupboard doors in my own house prevented me from expressing the opinion that the whole lot ought to have been surplus to anyone's requirements. After all, just because I can't see any use for the hundreds of cake tins and kitchen gadgets she has garnered over the years, it doesn't mean to say that they're any less worthwhile than my own topshelf collection of moletraps, purse-nets and the left-hand sides of a hundred sets of hames from long-forgotten harnesses. I know that all these will come in handy one day, so why shouldn't that umpteenth contraption of Mother's? I suppose we might even find a use for twenty-odd plastic lemons.

I hitch-hiked to visit the folks, and while Dad settled to a couple of hours' cricket, Mum and I tackled another roomful of unlabelled boxes. These contained a huge selection of what one might call toiletries. Soaps, lotions, sprays and scents. Lipsticks in colours that had no place on human faces. Tiny bottles of eau-de-skunk and great dredgers of talcum that brought tears to one's eyes and triggered off unsuspected allergies. Mum and I were in fits of giggles as we brought to light bottle after bottle of every woman's answer to everything from dandruff to sweaty feet, trying out a puff of this, a blast of that, until we smelled like a Hong Kong funhouse. We sorted it into piles, some to keep, some to throw away, some of the more outlandish make-up for my daughter to experiment with and some of the more conservative pongs for me to wear on my rare days out. I'm not one for great clouds of perfume, you understand, but have been known to boost my morale with a quick squirt of Je Reviens for special occasions.

We were in a rather weakened state when I found the tall blue bottle. It contained a sort of pearly cream, and it smelt rather pleasant. Mum asked what it was. Most of the label had been torn off, but what was left said' Crême de Bain'. 'Bath Cream' I told her. 'What's that?' she asked. But there she had me. I hadn't the faintest idea.

I felt as though I ought to know. After all, I once worked in the fashion and beauty department of *Woman's Journal*. But I didn't dare commit myself. It could have been an early version of the modern shower-gels, an alternative to soap for reviving the delicate tissues. On the other hand, it might have been a sort of up-market bath-cleaner. Mum suggested I take it home and find out.

I returned that evening with a carrier bag full of essences of another world. I set all the little bottles out in rows on dressing-tables and put the bigger ones in the bathroom. The tall blue bottle with the pretty cream somehow found its way into the kitchen, because I intended testing it on the tea-stains in the sink.

I saw it sitting there on the Monday morning when I returned to the harsh realities of our little farm. I was feeling depressed and miserable because it was time for Portia to go. She was heavy in-pig and therefore not likely to be consigned to the slaughterhouse, thus making the thing easier to justify. It was for the best that she should go to a new home, to avoid the overcrowding and underfeeding that occurs when we have too much livestock.

But I felt hollow and broken inside because I loved them all and, as always, suddenly loved best the one that had to go. I had now to clean her up for her prospective purchasers. It would be like washing a juggernaut. I had to remove all the winter's grime, the flaky skin, the piggy understains, and I wanted to treat her to a really special toilette. Pigs love being washed and scrubbed; they love massage and enjoy smelling nice. So out I went with wellingtons and waterproof trousers, a bowl of warm water and a stiff brush. And the tall, blue bottle of Crême de Bain.

I still don't know what it was really for, but it brought that pig up a treat.

With the money I got for Portia, I bought two pedigree Gloucester Old Spot gilts – thus giving the lie to my overstocking argument. I asked a fellow pig-keeper to take me to Todmorden to collect them and was delighted to see so many wonderfully piggy pigs, all spotted at random and no two alike. Dolly and Nellie were chosen, driven home in a Volvo, and stepped daintily into our lives with the minimum of fuss.

But around us the climate was changing. Pigs were popping up all over the place – several neighbouring farms had now got sows – and there were rumblings of the rivalry I had come to dread.

Rosalie having been the first sow in the dale for years, I felt sure that this time I would be at the head of the column, as it were – but there I was wrong. When it came to mating the gilts, I found it impossible to get the use of a boar pig – the available talent was 'booked', 'spoken for', 'not at liberty'.

So I bought Taffy. A young, handsome, hideously expensive Welsh boar. I justified this huge outlay by telling myself that I could lend him to my neighbours, thereby defraying a proportion of the cost. But nobody would use him, preferring to bring in the dealers' boar than to make use of the one who lived next door. And suddenly, I had a self-contained pig unit, just like that.

And when the time came for them all to farrow, the explosion of the pig population reverberated through the dale. Nellie, the first to go, started to produce her litter, before her milk supply came on line, as they say in the oil business, with the result that the little piggies came as a dreadful shock to her and she barked and snapped and drove them away from her, standing up to give birth so that they dropped one after another with a sickening thud on to cold concrete. After the seventh pig, I gathered up the newborns and put them in a box in the kitchen until the whole disastrous affair was finished, dressing the wounds of the worst-abused and comforting them as best I could. By the time Nellie had finished, her milk was there, and she nursed her last two piglets, crooning and muttering to them as tenderly as she had earlier cursed and ranted against their siblings. I put back the first seven and she took them to her bosom without reservation. But one of the worst-worried died the following day. Baby-battering in the farrowing-house – what next?

Dolly was next. She had plenty of milk and was already in the cuddly, gruntled state that a good mothering sow achieves prior to farrowing. It looked as though everything would be all right this time. But I did not dare depend on it until they were all safe.

And then it was Rosalie's turn. I can't remember whether it was the ninth or the tenth time, but once again she delivered herself of a handsome litter of good strong piglets. For the previous few days she had been subjected to repeated noisy and disruptive visits by Dolly and Nellie's little ones, who thought it great fun to call on Aunt Rosalie and tease her till she woke up, then scoot away with squeals of piggy merriment. At first she would gruff at them, which they seemed to find very amusing, but as her time drew nearer she became more tolerant until it seemed she enjoyed and appreciated their giggling company. They would clamber all over her vast bulk, sniffing under her ears and sliding off again into the straw, and all the while she would lie grunting quietly to herself.

It was an experiment I had longed to conduct, the establishment of a sort of family unit among my pigs. Now that there were three of them, and Taffy the boar, I wanted them to have a sort of community relationship – something of the kind one observes so frequently in nature and so seldom among one's fellow men. So when Nellie and Dolly were both safely farrowed and the little pigs were about a week old, I put all of them into one sty, with a piglet-size pophole in the door that separates the outdoor exercise yard from the rest of the farmstead.

Dolly and Nellie were let out twice a day for a drink and a

wander, though confined in my absence to their own joint quarters, but both litters of piglets could get out at all times to explore where they wished. That included Rosalie's next-door sty, which also is designed to let small pink persons in and out unrestricted.

Taffy was often let out, too, to walk with his children, and he was gentle and tolerant with them. The whole experiment proved an unqualified success, and has served to emphasise once again what I have known for a long time – that pigs are particularly pleasant people.

When Rosalie's farrowing became imminent, though, a wire mesh gate temporarily excluded the visitors from her sty. It wouldn't do for the bigger piglets to steal the first, special milk that nature provides specifically for newborn things, and for a day or two the old girl needed peace with her own treasured offspring.

I was popping in and out as they were coming into the world. Rosalie is used to my intermittent presence on these occasions, and is quite happy for me to share in her fulfil-ment. Strong little pigs arriving one after another at regular intervals. Some headfirst, some feetfirst, all with a sneezing, squealing desperation to connect themselves, like electrical appliances, to their one and only source of power, of life.

And suddenly it was Spring again. My underwear was full of hayseeds, my eyes full of sleep, and my bedroom full of cardboard boxes.

It began with Rastus. An unfamiliar car coming down the drive, a couple with a cardboard box and an apologetic air, and the orphanage opened its doors to the first of spring's casualties – a small black lamb. Rastus was a triplet. His mother had been so taken up with the other two babies that she had ignored him and he had been found the following morning stiff and almost dead. They had warmed him and fed him and then decided to bring him up to me, knowing of my fondness for foundlings. A gift.

And who would not have loved him? Lots of people, on reflection. He was damp and shining and had that strange aromatic smell that is special to newborn lambs. He was named at once after a hand-knitted understuffed teddy bear dearly loved by the children, that being the creature he most resembled.

And it was like going back to the beginnings again, and all the excitement of little lambs in cardboard boxes and sterilising feeding bottles and loving them and losing them and weeping for them when they died, and the sweet singing triumph when the apparently hopeless cases survived against all odds.

All around us Spring was going according to plan – Snuff's babies bounced behind her, and the two lambs I'd bought to rear on the goat's milk were strident and strong and three litters of piglets had joined us. Spring is the one promise you can rely on in this world where everything goes back on you, and somehow by taking care of the Rastuses I can say thanks for it.

Rastus mattered.

He mattered more than ever later that first night, when the first signs of bacterial infection gripped him. He shivered uncontrollably in the box by the fire, and his mouth watered constantly. He did not want to eat, his feet and ears were cold.

Since I first started collecting orphans, though, I've learnt a great deal, and I had an impressive array of equipment to draw on. I knew what was happening inside his little body and how to help him fight it. With modern antibiotics and old-fashioned laxatives. With warmth and regular feeding and love, without which the rest of it is a series of meaningless and expensive luxuries.

Before the week was out, disaster struck again. Because of the infra-red lamps in the pigsties and the electric fire for Rastus, the burden on the meter was too great. While I was out getting some groceries, the money ran out and the babies were left in the cold for God knows how long. Rastus was quite all right, and so were the pigs, all but one. She had squeezed under her brothers and sisters for warmth and was limp and lifeless.

I took her into the house and revived her, determined not to let her go because she was the smallest, the only one we could pick out among 21 identical piglets. It was folly to put her back with the rest in case it happened again. So I got her a box and put her inside in front of the fire, but she was lonely and still cold. As I fed her at bedtime I cuddled her, enjoying her tiny strength. Poor little thing, if only she had a wool coat like Rastus's . . . like all good ideas, it was that simple.

If you had looked into my bedroom, you'd have seen a cardboard box by the fire and in it the smallest, sweetest little pig you ever saw curled up asleep beside a tiny black lamb who rested with his eyes shut, sighing deeply . . . and with his head on a pink satin pig-pillow.

Then I broke the habit of a lifetime and bought a lamb in the auction ring at Northallerton. He was a bargain. I fell in love with him at first sight. He stood in the ring, the centre of a crowd of fat, scampering pet lambs. His ears dropped and he shivered. His naval cord still hung below him, looking like the string on a burst balloon, and when the auctioneer asked for a bid, there was a sort of silence. Pet lambs were so brisk a trade that year that I was unable to buy many, even privately, but little Sextus set me back one pound fifty and not many people thought he'd survive; they hinted as much as I set off for home with the sorry little bundle tucked under my jacket. I called him Sextus because he was the sixth lamb to be sold and, to identify him for collection, the Mart staff had sprayed a vast six on his tatty wool. The following week lots of people asked after him and seemed genuinely surprised that he had lasted till then.

Diana, though, seemed to take it for granted that he would survive. Diana took everything for granted. Diana was the name I gave to the little pig who now shared a plastic dustbin with Rastus, unashamedly making use of him as a woollen warming-pan. But it was only a temporary measure.

Rastus began to thrive, and then to grow. Not prodigiously at first, but noticeably enough to make him begin to look at little out-of-place in a plastic dustbin. He became lively, standing on his hind legs and peeping over the rim, chatting to Sextus, who had moved into the next-door bin. It began to look like the early stages of a rehearsal of *Endgame*. And at last Rastus managed to jump out. It was time for him and Sextus to go and live in the outbuildings, where there were two more lambs to play with. I took them out and they settled at once.

Not so Diana. She began to scream, loudly and insistently. She wanted Rastus. I tried to comfort her as best one may comfort a small pig, but the more I tried, the more she screamed. How could I explain to her that Rastus was a real live lamb, and not a piglet's teddy bear? I didn't. I simply went and fetched an elderly jumble-sale teddy whom I had adopted in a similar spirit to that which had prompted me to buy Sextus. I put him in the dustbin with the little pig, and she was perfectly happy, shoving the old bear about to her heart's content.

Wouldn't it be nice if all problems could be solved as easily as those of the very young?

I mentioned Nellie's aberrant behaviour at her previous farrowing to a friend who told me that this unease is fairly common among farrowing sows, and that the way round the problem was to give the sow a couple of pints of beer, just to settle her down.

I liked it. The idea, that is, not the ale! All the pig books suggested barbarous things like farrowing crates and summary dispatch to the fatstock mart. I made my mind up even before that first litter had been sold that next time I would

ply Nellie with strong drink and see her sail through her time
of trouble on a cloud of euphoria. Weeks before, I bought a
four-pint bottle of Hintons best bitter which sat on our
windowsill until it was needed. One or two people did ask
me what I was going to do with it if the pig didn't drink it,
but I said we'd cross that bridge when we came to it.

She drank it all right. It was late at night when I went out
to see Nellie that I decided the time had come. She had been
fussing and re-arranging her bed since teatime, and now a
gentle stroke of her udder would send her toppling sideways, crooning to non-existent piglets, while warm milk
trickled over the back of my hand. I decided I'd slip Nellie a
dormitory feast of pig meal, and poured the beer over it like
gravy on a Yorkshire pud. I hoped she'd like it.

She loved it. The very smell seemed pure pleasure to her,
and she sank her snout beneath the foam, sucking it up like a
pink elephant, and it not touching the sides of her on its way
down.

Now had that been the only part that pink elephants
played in the story, I would probably have spent that night
in bed, in the arms of Morpheus for want of anyone better,
and dreaming of warm things. But in the small hours I was
suddenly wide awake with that deep certainty that all was
not well. I was up and half dressed before my fuddled brain
focussed on what it was that had woken me, but gradually I
became aware of an intermittent noise like the crashing of
saucepans and I could make out hollow thumps, punctuated
by a sound like quiet cursing. Nellie was out!

I fled outside to find that she had been blundering round
and round the small enclosed yard outside her sty, and had
somehow managed to shut the wooden door and lock herself out. She was wet and muddy and extremely cross. She
staggered stupidly back into her sty and stood looking at me,
as nearly cross-eyed as a pig could be, and broke wind
loudly. Then she staggered past me out of the door and
wandered round the yard again, with the silliest grin on her

face, and I chased after her, determined to put her back where her warm, dry farrowing-place was waiting. Each time I caught up with her she stopped, leaning on me blissfully and it was like trying to push a juggernaut whose brakes had seized on. Then off she went again.

At last I got her back to bed, and sat with her till she fell into a sound and snoring sleep, but what would happen next I really didn't know. I had always been brought up to believe that no good would come of strong drink, and having spent a night administering comfort to a drunken sow, I'm inclined to agree. But the following morning eleven pigs slid into the world without violence, so now there'll always be a bottle on hand when such an event is due.

The financial gains from the three-sow unit were great, but the overheads were more than I could manage. The price of grain went up, the value of pigs dropped and what had begun all those years ago as an extension of the family became a terrifying yardful of dependants. Still nobody wanted to share Taffy, so I was forced to sell him; I missed him.

Months later, when it was time to part with the last litters he had left with us, I was helping George and Sandra with their annual brucellosis test. I told them I had arranged the sale of the young pigs so that I could make use of the boar between his visits to their sow and another neighbour's.

'That's a profitable job, boar-keeping,' mused George. 'That's the job you want to be in, Missus,' and I couldn't recall when I had last felt such a strong desire to punch one of my fellow-men!

Woolgathering

My sheep are a source of pride and delight to me. I often wonder if this has anything to do with the fact that I never dreamed of them before I began to love them. My only preconceived ideas on the subject were based on Sunday-school texts and I developed my methods of shepherding accordingly. The main points of husbandry were gleaned from Virgil's Georgics and the poems of Vita Sackville West. But the expertise in their handling and the craftsmanship of the calling was learned first-hand from neighbours.

The dodding of ewes was one of the first tasks I observed.

When all the summer's grass and leaves and busy growing things seem to have stopped and dissolved themselves into a sort of glutinous gravy that makes outdoors damp and hazardous underfoot, and indoors much the same, we think twice about letting the dog out for an unsupervised run, fearing what he might bring back on his paws. We are afloat once more on the sea of soul-swallowing mud that turns winter farming into a kind of trench warfare, and the old homestead into a dark and steaming hovel, with little damp piles of things in corners that only that morning were clothes clean-on and fit to be seen.

Then I spend many hours dodding sheep. Not the most uplifting of jobs, but one I usually enjoy, because I'm good at it. I can remember when I first came here and saw one of my neighbours bent double and unusually intent on a ewe's hinder parts, I asked what he was doing, and his embarrassment struck him dumb. But I didn't know then what 'dodding' was for, and I don't suppose many of you will – so here's the explanation. At this time of year the tups are loosed among the ewes to ensure the annual increase that follows in five months' time. All automatic, you might think, with nature taking its course and all that. Not so.

Between the tup and the particular part of the ewe that occupies his attention at these times is, in the case of the moor breeds, rather a lot of wool. So the hill shepherd removes it. If you go for a ride over the moors in late autumn you'll probably see the results of his work. The top of the ewe's tail and the heavy woollen breeches on her hind legs are clipped out and left shining like the gold on an archery target. Over the years I've lived here, I've become something of an expert.

But this year, I was helping Jim from Next Door with a hundred-odd ewes and we had only done about a dozen apiece when it started to rain. Having started, we decided to finish. Bent double over a sheep's bum, with icy water trickling down the back of my neck, I did wonder briefly whether this was indeed part of the plan that Providence had drawn up for me, all those years ago.

As I learn more about the annual tasks connected with sheep, a whole series of pictures spring to life, before and behind me, like a cartoon remembered from my childhood. A small man in a barber's chair, the assistant holding a mirror to show him the back of his own head – 'There you go, sir, – travelling at the speed of light into infinity. . . .'

Shearing time especially has become a fistful of memories, from the earliest days, when I first held one of Jim's old ewes with a throbbing left arm, in which the muscles strained to bursting even before I had poked the points of the too-new shears into the ruff of wool round her neck. One of the most difficult aspects of shearing is the control of the sheep, and for my first few seasons I found this hard to master. The actual snipping-off of the wool is as child's play beside the difficulties of holding on one-handed to a big strong ewe who seems suddenly to have recalled a pressing engagement elsewhere.

I remember how it felt when I first began to master the combination of the two skills. The hoggs, or yearling sheep, are always clipped before the older ewes, their fleeces 'rise' earlier and they are generally considered 'better shearing'.

One particular year, I had saved up the clipping of our hoggs until I was really in the mood, because it's one of my favourite occupations and it seems to be over far too quickly. Mind you, not quickly enough for the big farmers who still love taking the mickey out of me, with such remarks as 'If they lose their jackets as slowly as that, they won't miss them!'

But I don't mind. I know I'll never be a gun shearer, but I do enjoy the actual feel of the job and when you have as few sheep as I have and nobody around to criticise, I don't see what's wrong with spinning the whole thing out as long as possible, with no interruptions or harassments to spoil the gentle click of the shears and the coolness of the fresh grease against the back of my hand.

That year, visiting friends watched, sitting in their parked car with the radio cassette player blaring out. Now normally I hate the pollution of the atmosphere by the ubiquitous transistor as much as I pity the car-bound visitor who cannot enjoy being outdoors without the noise. But this time I was allowed to choose the music and I was surprised at how much difference that made to my attitude.

I began with Beethoven's Sixth, most appropriate, as I made all ready and then started on young Pipsqueak, our growing tup, just as the slow movement began. I wondered how those big farmers would have felt if they could have seen me. Slowly, slowly, as the music poured like iced water, Pipsqueak lost his fleece and I didn't cut him once. The next six sheep took me the whole of the *Emperor* Concerto and the first part of Mozart's *Eine Kleine Nacht-musik* – but if you know the music yourself, you can gauge how my pace was beginning to hot up. If I hadn't run out of sheep I might have finished with the flight of the Bumble Bee!

We all went down to the house after that to clip Snuff. That had to be done because my visitor had bought her fleece from me the previous year and his wife had handspun it and knitted a sleeveless pullover. Sleeveless because she had run out of wool. Your average down-cross fleece would have furnished enough wool for two sweaters, but this first effort at handspinning had produced a yarn of variable thickness, punctuated with the occasional spiky lump-like inferior barbed wire – and its production had doubtless included a good deal of natural wastage.

Everard, in his sweater, posed for a photo beside Snuff, in her fleece, and then I set on to clip her so that I could make them a present of the wherewithal for the missing sleeves.

Peter and Paul, her lambs, had to be in on the operation, and were an unimaginable nuisance, upsetting Snuff and poking their whiskery noses in at irregular intervals. In the end I had to put them out of the kitchen, where I had decided to do the job.

When I let Snuff back to her feet she looked tiny, her black skinny legs all knobbly beneath her rough-ridged body. Peter and Paul, now as big as she, ran back into the kitchen. Paul ran to Snuff and dived beneath her for a quick swig, but Peter, after a moment's hesitation, ran to Everard and buried his snout in the fine, hand-knitted sweater!

That summer was a particularly good one. Other memories from it return to warm me.

A morning walk under the great beeches at the bottom of the wood, meeting the sun on its way. Great sloping fingers

of hazy light poked among the huge trunks, and in them little dustmotes hovered and shone. A fat squirrel, burning with curiosity, edged his way from tree to tree, getting bolder by the minute, until I coughed and he shot out of sight straight up among the branches. Plimsolled feet wet with dew. Bare legs stinging as the sun dried them. Able to go out without a coat so early in the morning. Able to go out without a coat at all. Summer at last.

I sang on my way back to the house to get on with the milking, and the cows' relieving themselves when they stood up to let me pass sounded like restrained applause.

It was like being a girl again, at Granny Bumpstead's, at the beginning of a summer holiday, with the prospect of long days full of what seemed life's greatest pleasures, from the morning's dewy mushrooms to the evening's gatherings round the last little piece of corn to fall to the old binder, waiting for the rabbits to run out, missing them on purpose with the cudgel I cut from the hedge.

Those days had stretched on forever into nights warm and noisy with little benevolent sounds.

At home waited two little girls whose working mum is a good friend. They had come to stay for a few days, and I hoped that they were finding the same magic that was in my lost summer days years ago. Now and again, when I heard peals of laughter from somewhere near the house, I remembered my city childhood and the restrictions it placed upon me, and I thanked God that there are still places where children can run free and play all day with dirty hands and straw in their hair. These two revered my daughter Nancy as I once stood in awe of the big girl who lived next door to Gran – Googie, with a fund of wordly wisdom beyond her years and hair an incredible shade of ginger.

I called one of my goats after her, because she was that self-same unlikely shade, and now I went to the building where goat Googie awaited me, gave her a hug, and led her outside to be milked. She never needed to be tied up or bribed with food. She had learned that if she gave up her milk without fidgeting, she would get her reward after milking was finished. The only privilege upon which she insisted was to be milked first. It was her right.

As the day everywhere was swinging into its stride, I got on with the breakfasts. Rosalie Pig waited fairly patiently for what I could not persuade anyone else to eat and on this particular morning it included half a jar of marmalade traded by the visitors for Snuff's last fleece.

I don't know if you've ever heard anyone Scottish talking about marmalade, but they have a very special way of doing it. Try for yourself saying the word with an attempted accent. To get it right you have to somehow leave out most of the vowels and squeeze it out between pursued lips – M'ld. Well, this was that sort of marmalade, the sort that took your breath away and dried up the inside of your mouth so that your lips pursed automatically when you pronounced its tart name. Ugh!

It had been in the house for a while, because Everard, who gave us the whole giant coffee-jarful of it, had made it himself, and had been staying with us. I tried. We all tried. I really love marmalade, especially home-made, and the good fellow had brought a selection of other varieties which were most palatable, but this stuff was, believe me, lethal, cleaving the tongue to the roof of the mouth in real Old-Testament fashion. I gave it to Rosalie, with the end of a brown loaf and her breakfast milk.

Later in the day, the two little girls came to tell me solemnly that there were worms in Pig's dish. I went to see. Hundreds of little brown shiny bits lay in the bottom of her dish, looking very wormish indeed. I investigated further, then called everyone to come and look. The dear pig had done her best with Everard's marmalade, but even she could not manage that dreadfully bitter peel, and had spat out every bit.

Over the years, my attitudes to sheep and shearing have changed, just as the attitudes of the people with whom I have shared the tasks, from whom I learned, have changed towards me.

A few years after that special summer, I had been promoted by circumstances to the rank of shearer, the children had taken my place in the catching-fold and it was clipping time again. My thighs were dotted with little black bruises and my fingernails were rimmed with filthy black grease that will later be extracted in great quantities from the wool I've clipped and cleaned up and perfumed to be sold back to me as handcream to repair the damage that I've done. But this time of year is inclined to make one philosophical. One Thursday I put in a full day's hand-shearing, alongside Jim who was using an electric machine, and when the day was over and I walked along behind the newly-shorn flock as we took them to the fields where they would stay till dipping-time, I saw that a satisfying number of them bore the obvious signs of having been hand-sheared. There's a completely different finish to a hand-sheared sheep that stands out a mile; a sort of quilted effect, looking like raised squares on the right side of the sheep and long, curving lines on the left.

No two ways about it, I'd done my fair share of those sheep. I went home, fell into bed and dreamed of my triumph. I was a bit stiff, right enough, when the alarm went on Friday morning, but I pottered round the livestock, stuffing food into hungry mouths, and although it seemed to take a bit longer than usual, I didn't stop to think why.

I reported back to Jim's farm, sharpened up my shears, caught my first sheep and bent to my work. The muscles in the back of my neck screamed in protest, and when I stooped to open up the wool inside her right thigh, I felt as though my back would break.

I dropped the sheep gently to the floor and knelt with my toe under her chin and my knee behind her head, leaning across to take the long sweeps from the back of her neck to the base of her tail. My arms felt numb and my fingers stiffened round the shears. And when I took hold of her shorn tail to lift her buttocks from the floor to clear the wool off the underside, I thought I would never hold her up.

The last move in my own personal shearing technique is the trickiest. I get up and pull the sheep up with me, sort of twiddling her round at the same time and flicking the fleece with my foot, so that she sits tidily on her sheared bottom and I can put in the last few long blows on her left side that finally free her from her winter woollies.

Never, never have I made such heavy weather of it as I did with the first sheep on that Friday morning. I had seized up totally, and my tally was sadly down for the day. But I spent Saturday and Sunday gathering in more sheep, and on Monday my rebellious sinews seemed to have bowed to the inevitable and I put in another good and enjoyable day.

During these few days, though, I sheared most of my own sheep, which had been gathered in along with my immediate neighbours – some of them during communal gathering-parties and some by me alone. The pile of wool grew: fat white fleeces, rolled up inside-out waiting to be packed in the great hessian 'wool-sheets' provided by the Wool Marketing Board. Off they all went, and back in return came a statement and a cheque. Nice, if it weren't for the fact that, among all the literature sent annually by the Board is a list of British Wool knitwear, available to me as a wool-producer at concessional rates.

It is a source of great sorrow to me that so far the cheque for all that good Swaledale wool, the recompense for a whole year's woolwork, has still never been quite enough to buy from them one Swaledale sweater – even at concession-ary rates. But I dreamed. Anyone, after all, can dream. One still evening, when I felt in exactly the right mood, I would shear Bella, the only ewe whose jacket I had not yet removed. She was to be my entry for the Golden Fleece competition. Together we had got far enough the year before to win a red rosette and a tin of sheep-dip at the local judging.

Who knows – maybe this year she would win and I would have my very own Swaledale sweater, specially made as part of the prize. Meanwhile, last year's rosette lay in a drawer, telling me that someone, at least, thought I was beginning to know a bit about sheep!

Even though I had now become one of the shearers, as far as my immediate neighbours were concerned, I was still 'the lad', since Jim and George had both graduated to electric shearing. Soon after I arrived in the dale, Jim had purchased an ancient petrol-engined machine, which he perched in the back of his geriatric Landrover and ferried to the sheep pens instead of driving all the sheep to the nearest power-point, as he does now.

The old petrol-engined machine was a link, a bridge between the go-anywhere freedom of hand shears, where a man could choose according to a change in the wind where he clipped each sheep – under a tree, in the middle of a field – and the electric power-packs that stay where they're put, the men in charge of the hand-pieces joined to them by the fat, swinging cables and the sheep wheeled into position by the catchers.

George fancies himself as a 'gun' shearer, and gets quite temperamental if inefficiency among the ancillary staff does less than justice to his batting average. He has been moved to verbal and even physical violence by this. For George, speed is of the essence.

Jim's a pretty good hand with the electric clippers – but I remember with fondness his first attempts with that old petrol-engined machine. For a day or two, as he practised in secret with me as his only witness, he was a lad again – fumbling and inept, and I was able to give back a little of the encouragement he had offered to my own tentative efforts with the hand-shears at about the same time.

We have all moved a long way off from those close and special days. Now in summer Jim's fold yard is transformed into a shearing-shed and George races against Jim, against himself – but not against me. As I clang and clatter and roll my sheep gently this way and that, I still present no challenge to the 'real' shearers, as they see themselves.

To the other women in the shed, though, I present a different picture, but they are comforted, I think, by the fact that I am still not doing the job exactly like their menfolk. On a good day, though, I can clip a ewe to every two of Jim's and it pleases me to recall to myself the sheep-shearing in *Far from the Madding Crowd*, where Bathsheba tells Gabriel Oak, who is shearing at his best to impress her, that he has completed the task in three and twenty minutes and a half – and that she has never before seen one done in less than half an hour.

I can now shear three sheep in three and twenty minutes. And when George mocks me for 'taking my time' as he slips off fleece after fleece, I smile to myself. I can never compete with him. I content myself with the secret knowledge that I can sure as hell knock Gabriel Oak into a cocked hat!

But now, too, there are in the dale a whole new generation of young shearers, raised with the new technology, who have cut their metaphorical teeth on electric clippers.

'We've got a visitor,' said Nancy. That could mean anything from a pig having wandered into the kitchen to her having found yet another flea on the dog. But it was young Colin, from the big farm across the river. 'Are you doing anything tomorrow?' he asked. Now when a bronzed, blue-eyed young fellow, with a crop of golden curls and muscles that really do ripple and don't just lie there and look at you, asks a question like that, there's only one answer. 'Why?' I asked warily.

He said he had a lot of sheep ready for clipping, and nobody to help him. Could I 'give him a day?' I agreed readily. Mind you, I'd have gone even if he'd been a one-legged Chinaman with halitosis and a leaning towards black leather. I needed a long, hard day's work among my favourite creatures.

All my own stock were fed and everything done and dusted – well, done anyway – by eight o'clock, and I set off across the fields to join Colin, who was gathering up the sheep. Together we drove them and their complaining lambs into the shed and left them there, gasping for breath, while we went to get ourselves ready.

Colin was clipping. I was catching the sheep for him, wrapping the fleeces and acting as general labourer. It was a pleasure to watch him work, the gentle whirring of the machine and the easy way he handled the sheep gave his part of the enterprise an air of relaxation that made a weird contrast with my own scuttling progress. First into the pen to catch a sheep, then haul it out of the pen and hang on to it with one hand while I fastened the gate to prevent all the others from stampeding out after it.

As soon as Colin had finished one, he would push the fleece to one side and I would hand him the next candidate, then skip across and roll the shorn fleece ready for packing. This involves cleaning up the fleece by removing any mucky bits and flicking off the stray whiskers where the machine has double-cut, then turning both sides into the middle and rolling it up towards the neck end, where the rough 'collar' which has hitherto framed the sheep's face is pulled out into a long 'rope', twisted like barley-sugar, wrapped one and a half times round the rolled fleece and tucked in to hold it all together, looking like a cowboy's bedroll, with the best part of the fleece, the shoulder-wool, shown to best advantage.

It's easy to say, but there's quite a knack to it, and since the only way I can do it is by kneeling down, by the time we stopped for a break, I was looking decidedly the worse for wear, with my jeans rolled up to my knees to make a soft pad to kneel on, my cotton singlet so covered with grease and wool that my chest appeared hairier than Colin's, and my lower legs plastered with grey-green sheep-muck, as was my backside, where I had sat back on my heels to tie up the fleeces.

The day was hot and humid, and the sweat ran down between my shoulder blades. Not the sticky, fussy sweat of a promenade concert or the London underground, but the real, cleansing sweat of hard, physical exertion that is almost too much, but not quite. Sweat expended for the sake of the job in hand and not to impress anybody else. Except perhaps me, because I needed it. Or Colin, because he deserved it. Or Colin's wife, because she works for my bank manager.

One of the hazards of day-to-day living in a country district is the occasional necessity of doing some of the everyday jobs by the side of the Queen's highway. One day I was helping to sort out some lambs for old Henry, half of which had to be taken up the road to the moor gate. I set off gaily and, after having persuaded the owner's dog that it was in order for them to be going that way, and that there was no necessity to turn them back again, I whisked them along in fine style, going flat out for the gate.

Too late I saw the Morris Minor and the elderly couple picnicking by the open boot and enjoying the countryside. There they sat on a tartan rug, poor dears, he with a sandwich halfway to his mouth, she manipulating the contents of a Thermos into its little plastic cup with intense concentration.

The half-hundred galloping gimmers bore down on them like the hordes of Attila the Hun, and there was nothing I could do about it. There isn't a word for that situation. 'Fore!' 'Timber!', 'Gardy-loo!' – none of them conveys to a somnolent gentleman that his egg-and-cress is about to be smitten from his grasp by a horde of stampeding Swaledales.

Had it been a sheepdog trial, I would have gained full marks for sending my charges unerringly between the two obstacles, neither of whom appeared to flinch as their smart rug was covered temporarily by another of best Yorkshire wool – on the hoof. I put the lambs out through the gate and returned to apologise. They insisted that they had enjoyed watching real country life at such close range and seemed genuinely disappointed that it was all over.

It was a similar incident that brought to light another gap in my rural education. I was assisting at a roadside clipping session and was conscious of the steady gaze of two lady motorists who had left their car and were watching the proceedings with rapt attention. They rested their bosoms on the top rail of the fence like privileged bottoms on shooting sticks and the larger one kept up a whispered commentary which ceased only when I shook out a particularly fine fleece prior to wrapping it up.

'Now that,' she declared loudly, 'is what I would like on my lounge floor.' I pointed out that this was a fleece and not a skin, and that a necessary part of her projected rug was still, for the most part, on the sheep and, as the smaller lady twinkled almost imperceptibly, the larger covered her obvious confusion by asking me with exaggerated interest how a sheepskin rug was made.

It was now my turn to cover my ignorance, I had no idea.

I had had abortive attempts at preserving rabbit pelts and moleskins with paraffin, which resulted in something which felt like a cross between textured floor tiles and mouldy crispbread, and their only use was as a breeding ground for one of the less choosy species of British fly. They were finally disposed of, along with the accumulated ground bait, on the bonfire.

But I have the large lady to thank for rekindling my interest. I sent away to a firm of taxidermists for a substance that would, they claimed, reduce the crispbread to softest suede, and purchased a quantity of formalin which would, I felt sure, when used as the first stage of the process, dissuade the maggot-mongers.

I was given the skins of two sheep sent for slaughter. These were left for me in the hut at the top of my hill one very foggy night. I groped up to collect them before the local cats did and felt, torchless, for a woolly pile in the darkness. I gathered together in my arms a fearful amalgam of harsh hairiness and cold, wet skin and wished I could see, but on the way down the hill I discovered that not only were they extremely heavy but that stiff, dangling things were knocking against my shins, and I was glad that I could not.

I staggered into the kitchen and dropped the red, wet ruins in a heap on the flags. I was daunted to see that so much had been left. All the feet were there, as were the ears and the muscular contrivances below the tail. I set to with a knife designed for trimming linoleum, removing all these together with the hairless areas of armpits, legpits and belly.

After an hour's work resembling a practical examination for a fellmonger's apprentice, I had a pile of bits in the middle of the floor and two fairly tidy skins. One of them was a medium-sized Swaledale, grey and lightly curled; the other was a huge Border Leicester whose purled ringlets shone like shavings of golden butter in the lamplight.

I mixed a five-per-cent formalin solution and soaked them for a week. Then I removed them, rinsed them, nailed them out on discarded doors and rubbed in a fistful of the new honey-coloured goo. After several weeks of finger-splitting effort I deemed them ready for the final stage – wash after wash in detergent solution in the bath until they were freed of all the sandy particles, bits of bracken and barbed wire that the normal sheep carries around. Then I stretched them out to dry naturally in the sun and as they dried I knew that the operation had been a complete success.

I did not brush them out afterwards, preferring that they should retain their individual characters. The Swaledale, coarse and homely, with its bird's nest of rough curls speaking of moorland mist and heather, back-to-the-wind on frosty mornings. The Leicester, rich and heavy, hanging with lustrous ringlets grown on clover leys and aromatic pastures.

Now I look forward to the next time a passer-by asks me how to cure a sheepskin. 'Well,' I shall say, settling myself for a protracted conversation, 'that depends on what ails it . . .'

In the years I've been keeping sheep there have been no end of innovations, especially in their feeding. Some of these ideas I have tried myself – like the self-feed molasses. Like most of the things I get myself involved with, it seemed like a good idea at the time.

With the winter starting so very badly, I began to give my sheep the goodies I had intended to save for the worst of the weather and then, when it turned mild and stayed mild, I began to wish I hadn't been quite so rash with the hand-feed. Even though the weather had improved, you see, it would be bad husbandry to withdraw the rations I had established.

That left me with the problem of what extra feed I could find for them now that the countdown to lambing had begun. A firm in Sedbergh offered a mixture of molasses and cider vinegar that sounded wholesome and delicious, so I bought them a few gallons. The next problem was how to get the black, sticky substance from the big heavy drums to the small heavy sheep. The answer, I was assured, was balls. Plastic balls.

The suppliers of the molasses supplied me with a nobby little effort which resembles a black plastic top hat. The idea is to take an empty plastic jerrican, make a hole in one side, put the top-hat brim-upwards in the hole with the ball stuffed in the crown like a magician's rabbit, and then fill the whole contraption with molasses.

Game for anything, I gave it a try. Make a hole, they said, but I found myself in a corner of the kitchen surrounded by sharp objects, none of which seemed designed for making holes in plastic jerricans, and experimenting half-heartedly with what was to hand. I broke the sawblade in the Stanley knife. I bent the potato peeler. My only penknife of the right shape folded itself up when I pressed on it, trapping my forefinger, and a chisel bounced off and broke a tumbler on the draining board. In the end I made holes with a screwdriver and joined them up with the breadknife.

Now I had to get it up to the place where I fold my sheep for the night, and fill it with molasses. It was a very windy day. Five gallons of anything takes some holding up and it's impossible to hit the little top hat with a steady stream of molasses when your arms are shaking with the strain and the wind is whipping the stuff into sticky strings that wind themselves round your legs. I went back for a jug and did the job in easy stages.

At last I had it filled, and the little plastic ball bobbled on top of the jerrican like a cherry on a bun and at a fingertip touch it rolled round and round, coating itself over and over again with the sweet, sticky mixture, like ink on a ballpoint pen. The air was filled with the smell of treacle-toffee. All I needed now was some sheep to try it out.

Several of my neighbours had introduced their sheep to these feeders and all reported success after their sheep got the hang of the thing. My sheep, I felt sure, would twig at once that they must lick the ball so that it would spin round and deliver mouthfuls of sweet nourishment. I let them in and they rushed to investigate. Lamb Chop, most intelligent of all the sheep, endowed with more than her fair share of cunning, tried it first. Up she went to the tried and tested foolproof feeder. She sniffed the ball, licked it and round it went. She licked it again. Then, clearly irritated by the erratic wobbling of her tasty treat, she trod firmly on it to hold it still. Down went the ball and a jet of molasses shot all over her. This didn't happen in the explanatory leaflet.

But the next day when I went up to look, they had all had a go, judging by the appearance of their sticky whiskers and by the colour of their drinking water, which looked like brown Windsor soup.

At the time of writing sheep farmers are in the grip of another compulsory dipping period, with all its attendant restrictions. That means much hard work and forward planning, but, however you look at it, it's better than being in the grip of an outbreak of sheep scab. I have never seen an actual case of the disease, but there are plenty of reports and pictures which leave little to the imagination and I'd do anything possible to spare my sheep the misery of that.

A few years ago there was an outbreak of scabies at our local comprehensive school, and several mothers had to cope with miserable itching children. We anointed them and dipped them and did all that we were advised by our doctors and the little beasts were soon under control (the skin-mites, that is, not the children!).

It seems strange that some people who keep sheep do not think it worthwhile to protect their charges from such acute discomfort, but the Ministry literature suggests that there are flockmasters who do not dip regularly, hence the need for the compulsory dippings, and spot checks by officials with stopwatches, with all the additional irritation that this bureaucratic interference causes. Not that we mind up here. Our local inspector is a lovely ex-policeman, and his happy face and intelligent conversation have enlivened many a long day's hard work round the dipping-tub in the yard.

Now and again I have dipped my sheep by themselves, using my own dip – that I won in the annual Golden Fleece competition – but it's always easier and more fun to join in with neighbours and make one of the communal days that are so rare nowadays, even on these little hill farms. The hill farmer nowadays is becoming one of the loneliest men on earth, taking over the traditional role of the lighthouse-keeper as one whose work separates him utterly from all human contact. Poor chap, he can't afford to employ another man (or woman, more's the pity) to share the workload of these smaller farms, so he buys the machinery that will enable him to cope singlehanded, and away he goes in his safety-cab like the ancient mariner. Alone. Even the sons of these farmers can't stay at home and share the work, because there isn't enough income to support two families in the way the western world in general has come to expect.

So when there comes a chance to share in one of these rare days of communal activity, I grasp it with both hands and savour every moment, even when the work is hard and dirty, the weather hot and humid and the conversation limited to aspects of shepherding. Each sheep has to be caught, carried to the edge of the tub, and dropped in. Few submit quietly. Last time, I ended up with bruises in places I had forgotten I had; but the sheep were all dipped satisfactorily, nobody had lost their temper, and for a whole day people talked to one another instead of waving, albeit cheerfully, from some vehicle or other.

As usual, we discussed the merits of different dipping facilities, in particular the newer 'walk-in, walk-out' tubs that have much prominence in the farming papers. The advent of such a thing in the immediate vicinity would do away with yet another of the few labouring tasks remaining for the likes of me. In theory. But I've learned a bit about sheep since I've been living here, and while I have no doubt such an arrangement would fool a hill ewe once, or even twice, I am prepared to bet it wouldn't persuade one of the older ewes, facing the water music for the third or fourth time. Only human determination can do that.

There are other times, though, when sheep farmers still come together, though these get fewer and further between as progress insulates them from each other. Like the annual sheep-sales, erupting in October all over the hills, the last lingering echoes of Hardy's 'Pummery Fair'. Sheep are driven in wagons nowadays, rather than droves, but come they still do and these days still have a kind of grubby

Yorkshire magic, not only in the great accumulations of sheep but in the occasional coming together of like-minded individuals.

One such day must speak for all. It's terribly early. There's nothing but limp darkness outside and the pigs haven't woken up yet to oink at the door for their breakfast. The day is still a bit creased and damp at the ends, like Nancy's clean blouse which I've hung over the cooker on a nail. It will be ready by the time she gets up, by the time the working parts of the countryside have at last swung into gear, prodded into action by the rosy-fingered dawn, as it were.

I can't help wishing there was some porridge. It's a time of day that was never designed for yogurt. Most people probably have the impression that dwellers in the country, especially farmers, are up and about at this hour every day. I expect you have visions of apple-cheeked milkmaids tripping through the morning dew and farmers' wives thrusting trays of seething dough into warm and waiting ovens. I know I did, and it's part of the reason why I get up early-ish in the normal course of events. It's all part of one's image of the country gentlewoman. But in the interests of accuracy, it would be as well for you to know that if you and I were to go for a walk before seven, we'd find the hillside dew-pearled, sure enough, but I can guarantee we'd have it all to ourselves!

Times have changed since those days. British Summertime and television have stretched the day out of its old shape. After all, a man can't be up betimes if he's sat it out to the end of the Big Film, and there's precious little point in setting off across the fields to find stock in total darkness, especially since the greater proportion of hill cows are black!

Mind you, the day I am describing is the annual exception. It is the morning of the Swainby Sheep Sale, a great even in the North Yorkshire calendar, and that's why I'm up myself even earlier than usual. There's a lot to do, if I want to be ready to hitch-hike to the sale field with the locals, and I must be there to help load the first trailers from Jim's farm if I want a lift there for old Pipsqueak.

The little pet lamb who grew up to serve in the capacity of tup for our flock of Swaledales has done his two years, and in the interests of genetic hygiene I must find him a new home, a new flock to serve. It is the turn of last year's pet lamb, Rocky, to take over the leadership.

I don't suppose Pip will make much of a price in the face of pedigree opposition, but after all there will be others there who want a strong hardy stockgetter, even if only to 'chase', after the sheep are back out on the moor and the more expensive tups are retired to the in-bye for the winter. Pip won't mind. He's eager to do the job he loves, bless him!

And I'm not the only one who'll be up sooner than usual. All over the dale there'll be farmers with flashlights, rattling buckets and hunting for ewes and tups that have appointments with the auctioneer and who, with true animal perversity, will be as far as possible from the loading-places. Tempers are often more than a little frayed on Swainby Day, and the first sounds of the morning are more often muttered threats and mild profanities than the sweet sounds of birdsong, which run them a pretty poor second.

If the people who hear the tales of the ancestry of the mighty tups at the saleground could hear, as I do, the opinions expressed thereupon during the gathering and loading processes, they'd perhaps have their eyes opened!

How glibly, as a city child, I sang of *The Derby Tup*, whose physical attributes were utterly beyond credibility, even in their expurgated version. It was not until I had left school that I heard the last verse:

> The man who sold the tup, boys,
> Grew very, very rich –
> But the man who told the story
> Was a lying son-of-a-bitch. . .

And not until I had tasted the special flavour of Swainby did I realise that, around the sale ring, all tups are described with that same straightforward mendacity, and even the York-shire hill farmer, usually laconic to the point of churlishness, suddenly displays the inspired braggadocio of the East-end market trader.

A man who, to my knowledge, always ran eight un-marked tups with his moor flock, would give minute details as to the progeny of the one he happened to be selling when he had no means whatsoever of ascertaining which they were. 'Aye, but t'owd bugger gets bonny gimmers' was one such claim and the auctioneer took it up delightedly. A younger farmer, catching on fast, claimed that his tup had left him some grand wether lambs. 'Gets wethers, does he?' howled the auctioneer. 'Now that'll be worth a shilling or two, gemmen. . . .' and the crowd guffawed.

All sorts of outstanding business is concluded at Swainby; debts are settled and arguments rekindled – some of which will have been simmering since the last sale. Three rings operate at once, in the tradition of the best of circuses, and ewes, lambs and tups change ownership and are loaded and unloaded in a great woollen coming-and-going that weaves among the sideshows that the drug companies and handling-equipment salesmen have set up in tents and caravans around the main goings-on. And more often than not it's pouring with rain.

I can remember my first visit, being delighted by what I saw, yet apart from it all, as if I were walking through an educational hologram. I can remember what it felt like being the outsider, the entertained, like a child at a pantomime.

I remember George, strutting, taking the snout of one of his father's tups in his hand, digging his nails in, squeezing, laughing, wagging the patient head from side to side, saying '*Now*, then, how are you?', and shouting angrily when I asked him to stop, 'It's not thine. When it is – then thou can give thy bloody orders!' I cried then, though later I saw his outburst not as an attack but a defence.

That was a long time ago. A year or two later I was entrusted with the selling of Old Henry's draft ewes and took to task a drover who had split the lip of one of them with a length of alkathene pipe, because she had tried to bolt back on the way to the ring. He cursed me and waited for me to crumble. I cursed him back.

I've bought tups there, bidding with almost unbearable selfconsciousness, and sold them, enduring the auctioneer's jibes with masochistic pleasure.

And I will face them again in the same spirit – cherish them as part of the joys of belonging; of being one who may be asked – '*Now*, then, how are you?'

It's Swainby Day and I wouldn't miss it for the world.

'One of your sheep is out on the road,' said a passing neighbour. 'Right-oh, I'll see to it,' said I. And there began one of the longest, maddest chases I'd ever conducted, all along the road at the top of our hill, in and out of people's gardens, over walls and under wires, into old Henry's outside lavatory and out again over his winter fuel-pile, with coal cascading everywhere as I grabbed, missed, and we both set off again, the unfathomable in pursuit of the unbiddable, as it were, with all the excitement of the hunt crowned at last with success as I finally cornered the thing behind the roadman's garage and dragged it into the light of day to admonish it severely for having been so foolish as to escape and then so uncouth as to avoid capture, leading me such an undignified dance in the process.

I made my voice gruff, but loud enough to be heard by any inquisitive neighbour thus obviating the need for explanation and took a good look at the sheep so that I might address it by name. It stunned me to realise, slowly and only after a full minute's staring, that I simply couldn't put a name to it. A few moments later, I realised that this was because I couldn't have put a face to it either – it wasn't one of mine.

It belonged to the road-man – that's why it had been so singularly unresponsive to my call; so eager to evade my loud and lumbering pursuit. But after I had put it back in his field, patched the hole in the net and wandered halfway home again, I stopped to think about what had happened.

It hurt, like poking your tongue into the cavity of an aching tooth, but I stabbed away bravely. It was not only humiliating to have spent so much time chasing a sheep that turned out not to be mine; what made me feel really uncomfortable was the fact that I thought it was, simply because it might well have been. I have so many more sheep than when I began. So many new, young ones, daughters and granddaughters of the beloved founder-members – and I had secretly dreaded the day when they became strangers to me. And now it had happened.

Of course, there was every reason why I should not recognise this sheep – I didn't know it, never had. If the poor ewe had anything to do with it, I never would. But then, neither had I known that it was a stranger – and I should have done. Time was when it would have been apparent simply from the way a sheep walked, the way she held her head, whether she were mine or not.

I went back to my own small field, reclaimed from the roadside bracken-patch, and called my sheep to me, trying to count them while they jostled and jumped, whiskery snouts up my sleeves and in my pockets – but here and there one or two aloof, younger sheep. A bit distant. Cool and reserved.

'Better for it', my farming neighbours would assert – but I wasn't so sure. I felt again that heavy sadness that has dogged me lately. The sense of having lost touch with something important. Somewhere there is something I have forgotten, something I have mislaid. And I want it back before it's too late. I have almost become a farmer, but I am not quite sure if that's what I really want; if it does not ask too big a sacrifice.

I touched the remaining treasured faces and thought about it. Is this loss more mine than theirs? Perhaps so; but whatever it is, it is a loss I felt deeply. And I want it back.

O Rare Turpin

I kept him for his humour's sake,
For he would oft beguile
My heart of thoughts that made it ache
And force me to a smile.

WILLIAM COWPER

From the earliest stirring of memory, there was always a dog
at my feet. When I was two or three, and living with my
mother's mother, Granny Davenham, while my parents
found somewhere to live in London, I was taken to see a film
with 'Lassie' in it, and my first animal companion was thus a
rough collie, with more intelligence than all the humans
around me ever gave either of us credit for. I can see that dog
to this day, sitting watching me as it used to do at Granny's.
It sits with its aristocratic head slightly to one side, its little
eyes like currants in its snipy face. One foreleg is raised, a
thin paw hanging delicately from a limp wrist, like a canine
queer. I cannot now understand why I thought it beautiful,
but since none of the adults in my life could see it, even when
it was at my heels, I never had to justify its appearance to
anyone.

Granny knew that it was there, because I told her, and she
leapt into the fantasy with an enthusiasm that had not yet
begun to embarrass me. She must have brought my parents

into the secret, because before I went to join them in London, they had purchased a real dog for me. I can remember Granny reading aloud a letter from my mother, telling me about it. Mother was asking what we should call the puppy, and Granny quoted 'shall it be Lassie?'. She looked hard into my face, waiting for joy to appear, and I expect she saw it. Common-sense tells me that at that age I could not have interpreted this well-meaning conspiracy as anything at all sinister. It was only in adolescence that I began to see it as a sort of betrayal.

For the dog waiting for me when I returned to London was not the devoted soul-mate I had dreamed of – nor did it look as though it might be, even in the fullness of time. It was smooth, black, small and, in latter years, gross of form and uncertain of temper. All this, I know, I could have woven into my dog-fantasy for, young as I was, I had already grasped the principles of compromise. But poor 'Lassie' was utterly devoted to my mother. This I eventually accepted but could never quite forgive.

The passing of Lassie was thus not the traumatic experience it should have been. My parents had her painlessly destroyed a few days after the birth of my sister. The poor old creature was in constant rheumatic pain and the decision was the only one possible – but still I wallowed in the self-pity that came when I forced myself to recall that it was no more mine than the dog had been, and there was a sort of sombre triumph in the acceptance of it all.

In the early days of my marriage, there was Karl, an Alsatian who represented one of my husband's fantasies. I remember him with affection, because he no more lived up to what was expected of him than I did. Thus one of the things most looked forward to when the marriage ended and the numbness wore off and was replaced first by determination and then by real excitement, was the choosing and the having, for the very first time, of a dog of my own.

There were two border collies – Cap and after him Ruby –

who seemed, as puppies, more than likely to become the dog I felt I lacked, but both grew away from me, both proved untrustworthy. Both were, of necessity, confined to a degree that disgusted me deeply – I could not grant either of them, as adults, even the most limited of freedom, knowing in my heart that they would abuse it, Cap by harming people, Ruby by tormenting livestock. It was my failure, I knew, and my guilt ached each time I fastened them up, knowing that they would forgive, that they would greet me each time I went to them with no recriminations, no complaints. Each day I would be granted a clean slate, and each day I would soil it by fastening the dog once again in the kennel that had no place in my dog-dream.

Local farmers, who are in the habit of fastening their dogs by a collar and chain, found my attitude to this confinement surprising. But their dogs were employees. This was in their contract. When they were not chained, they were working, serving the one person in whose presence they were whole, doing the work of generations of their kind. I was totally unable to train either of these two dogs, possibly because I listened to too much advice, and their lives seemed limited to a degree to which I could not reconcile myself.

Cap met with an accident, kicked in the head by a cow he was harassing, and Ruby, named after a favourite aunt, died three years later after eating a packet of slug pellets I had put in what I believed to be a safe place. I wept for both of them, but their deaths were, in some measure, a relief to my conscience.

With Cap I had made a brave effort to do things by the book. James Thurber once wrote a piece about a dog whose only distinction was his tendency to bite people. I remember laughing a good deal when I read it. I wonder if I can find a copy of that article to show to Mrs A. who took Cap and me to the sheepdog training class and who was rewarded for her kindness by being involved in an unlady-like tug-of-war as we tried to separate Cap and her Pip, who seemed determined to fight to the death until we stopped the bout in round one and persuaded them to call it a draw; but they were obviously eager for a return match, and I withdrew miserably to a safe distance, delivering a public warning that was more for the benefit of my battered self-confidence than the dog's education and I was prevented by sheer cowardice from rejoining the chattering group of dog-handlers by the fence.

Cap looked up at me. With his dark sloe eyes and his odd ears, one of them pricked expectantly, the other permanently collapsed, his was a face that only blind bias could call lovely, but affection made it almost acceptable. This unpredictable violence accorded ill with the dog who could take tiny crumbs from between my lips without ever catching me with those formidable teeth.

The making of a sheepdog, some say, is in the breeding, but personally I have a sneaking suspicion that the breeding of the handler has more to do with the results than the breeding of the dog.

This was the first time I had set my sights on a real target – to train the dog who would help me in my faltering steps towards my own flock of moor sheep. Not so much a sheepdog as a guide dog. Not so much a guide dog as the blind leading the blind. . . . Such were my thoughts as I wandered miserably at lead's length from the rest of the group.

A nice young man with a new dog, bought ready-trained from an expert, talked to me for a while but when he confided how much the dog had cost I wrapped the lead round my hand once or twice and lengthened the distance between us. If Cap bit her head off I could never pay the damages.

I felt like a Sunday soccer player in the middle of a first division game. Like two pennorth of eels without any jelly . . . Then Cap, eager to regain my favour, dived wildly and returned with something in his mouth. It was a stick. We often went wooding together, Cap and I, and he knew a bit of good kindling when he saw it. With ill grace I stuffed it hurriedly into my pocket, but not before the rest of the group had seen. And commented. I tried to make excuses for him. To get to the field where we stood, with the wind whipping itself into a frenzy and driving the inevitable rain far enough into us to dilute our bone-marrow, Cap had had to endure his first-ever ride in a motor vehicle. Perhaps this had upset him, especially since he had been put in the boot. But suddenly I wasn't sure. Not sure about my dog. Not sure of anything except that I wanted to go home.

At the first lesson, after Cap had gone wild among the sheep and chased them until they could hardly move, the instructor had told me that I must concentrate on being able to put the dog down and rely on him to stay there until I called him. He said I should master this before we could go on. So I mastered it. All through the weeks that separated the two occasions I had practised until I could take him and put him down two or three fields away and then call him back and I was proud of this. To tell the truth, which I always try to do, I couldn't wait to show the instructor.

I had had the distinct feeling that he didn't think much of my command of Cap at our first meeting, and I had to admit that it was a rather haphazard kind of relationship. I had spent so much of Cap's life instilling in him that dogs leave other people's sheep alone that it was clearly going to be hard to communicate to him that we now had sheep of our own and he could, with guidance, work them.

It was the guidance that caused the difficulty. That was what I had really come for – to learn how to show him what I wanted him to do. I had learned lesson one well, and hoped for praise as much as Cap did. I had told Mrs A. on the way that I could put Cap down anywhere and I believed it, but suddenly I had grave doubts.

The wind howled and my feet and fingers numbed. We were to go last, the instructor said, after the Pip incident, and he said it was because the sheep would have quietened down by then, but I had a sneaking suspicion that he wanted to be sure there would be some sheep left for Floss, Nell, Ken and the rest to work on. When it was finally our turn I heard Mrs A. telling the others that I had said I could get Cap to lie down anywhere, and suddenly it sounded silly. 'I can do it at home,' I said hastily, and that sounded childish. I don't blame them for laughing.

As the three of us trailed across the field to where the sheep were, I told the instructor that I had been doing as he had said. He told me to put the dog down, and so I did. Down he went, bless him, and sat steady as a rock until I whistled him back. I did it twice more. The instructor was impressed and I responded to his praise with a warm inner glow. If I had had a tail, it would have wagged. But not for long.

When I tried to get Cap to go round the sheep, he still sat like a rock until given the release command, when he ran to my side and ignored the sheep completely. At one stage the instructor was poking him with a stick and urging him to run, while his eyes followed me across the field, pleading with me to explain what it was he was supposed to be doing next.

After a few more abortive attempts the instructor said to me that he was at a loss to know how we could get Cap to run and my heart sank – after all, that was the secret I was expecting to be told. 'A bull-staff,' suggested the instructor, 'or anything that would push him right or left . . .'. I thought miserably to myself that I could always throw a stick.

On his next visit to the class, he bit the instructor savagely. We did not go again.

Cap never learned to work sheep; I never learned to trust him until the day he died.

Ruby, given to me to replace him by neighbours who still had a little faith in me, was somewhat less of a burden, but

her devotion to me amounted to a jealousy that was a threat
to the children, who were afraid of her.

She, too, had to spend most of her days in an outbuilding,
but her life was not entirely without its good moments. The
fact that these were the exception rather than the rule,
though, points out yet again my failure to form a relationship with a dog that would satisfy the need that was still
somewhere inside me, left behind from the lost and lonely
days of childhood make-believe when I was still sure that my
dog – like the lover who replaced it in later fantasies – would
somehow find its way into my life.

I still wanted my dog as badly as ever, and still believed
that it was somewhere, waiting to be found.

But it wasn't Ruby, although at some special times she
came very near, and on one particular day, I almost felt that
we had found one another.

It was a sleepy, golden noon of the sort that has no
business to be about in November, but was no less welcome
because of that. I had been working since morning on a long
and boring job and felt that I had earned the right to saunter
among the creatures and lean on the gate to count my
blessings while the sun warmed the back of my neck and
drew the daydreams up into my head like a pleasant
poultice.

I let Rosalie Pig out into the orchard and gave the fading
trees a few hefty swipes with the clothes-prop. Great bliz-
ards of plums stotted down on to her piggy corpulence and
burst among her bristles. She crunched greedily. I used to
worry about turning her loose among the fallen plums
because I wondered what she would do with the stones. I
was sure that to swallow them would do her damage. I need
have had no fears; she grinds them to innocuous bits before
they go down so her appendix, if she has one, is not threatened. I used to worry about the goats, too, but observation
proved that, although they swallow the stones whole, they
regurgitate them along with their cud, and spit them out as

neatly as any upper-crust diner in little piles beside them. I once watched one of my goats nonchalantly spitting stones while a tiny mouse – or possibly a succession of tiny mice, wheeled them away one by one to nibble out the kernels in private.

Then I thought it would be a good idea to give Ruby a bit of gathering practice with the sheep around the house. I let her out and we set off together to see what we could see. Not a lot, as it happened, because as we set off down the field I was aware of pounding feet behind us and turned to see Rosalie at full gallop coming to join us. I was going to take her back and fasten her up, but she was so excited about the prospect of spending some time with me and with Ruby, whom she adored, that I relented and decided to take the pair of them for a walk.

Down the broad path and into the dark and secret silence of the beechwood we went, my companions shoulder to shoulder, one step ahead. Now and then Rosalie would stop, snout for a moment into the brackens underfoot, then rummage furiously for some goody or other. Ruby would join her, enlarging the hole and sending great clods of black leafmould flying over her shoulders while Rosalie watched in admiration. Now Ruby would go ahead, turning to scuttle back when she realised she was alone, now Rosalie would lag behind and squeal for us to wait, thundering after us with her ears clapping together above her head with every plunge. I sat down for a while in the sunshine that filtered through the branches of the turning trees. Both creatures returned to my side and Rosalie lay across my knees while Ruby sat at my shoulder, licking both of us in turn.

Then we set off again, and I noticed that the sides of my face felt odd and it was a ridiculously long time before I recognised that this was because I was smiling as I walked along, just happy. Suddenly, as I watched my two friends, I remembered something I once said to a schoolfellow of mine. We were trying to find the loveliest thing we could wish on anyone, like the fairy gifts the sleeping beauty was given. We tried health, wealth, happiness and all the usual ones, when I suddenly thought of 'May all those you love, love one another', and here I was reminded again how pleasurable is that state of affairs, and, in human terms, how rare.

Isn't it sad that when we become conscious of being happy, we begin to question it, to seek to improve it? Suddenly I wished that I had someone to share the gaiety with, someone to show the daft antics of dog and pig, someone to retell it all to, someone to reflect it off so that I could enjoy it all again through someone else's eyes. I decided to go back to the house for the camera, to capture and hold this strange, enjoyable experience.

Ruby and I left Rosalie digging but when we returned with the faithful family Brownie I laughed to see her galloping round the woodland tracks like a car at Brands Hatch, leaning over on the corners and squealing like a little boy pretending brakes, desperate to find us again. But you can't capture such speed on a Brownie 127, so I waited for more pictures to present themselves. But they didn't. Somehow the awkwardness of the little black box prevented it. Each time I raised it to capture something sudden and silly, Ruby would stop, look puzzled, and trot back to me to see what I was doing. Both they and I were self-conscious, and my left eye began to ache with the effort of holding it shut as I peered at everything, all diminished and second-hand, through the viewfinder.

It was when I finally lost my temper with Ruby and roared at her to lie still that I realised that I was spoiling everything in a futile attempt to keep it. I remembered with shame the restraining hand I placed on Nancy's shoulder when she ran to pick a late, solitary clover flower. Leave it, I told her, for finding is sometimes better than keeping. I explained that the clover flower, such a happy surprise in the rough grass at the corner of the meadow, would be a grubby nothing by the time it was back at our house, pulled from a pocket and cast aside. Sometimes, I explained, true and total possession of things is only gained by permitting their continued existence outside the limits of our restricting grasp. The true photographer has a gift that is denied me, as have the many painters who station themselves on the hill tops putting on to canvas a delicate blend of what they are seeing and what they are feeling. Both of them, at their finest, add a little of themselves to what they seek to carry away with them, making it worth sharing with others.

I lifted the tatty cord over my head and hung the camera on a holly twig. I turned and left it there, and suddenly the afternoon came to life again, just as it had been before. Ruby stood, poised for a moment in a patch of tawny sunlight, one paw raised and her beautiful head slightly turned on one side. A perfect picture. But suddenly I was glad I no longer had the camera with me. It could never have caught the memories of the scruffy pup, the feel of satin fur under languid fingers, the mud that had been on the end of her nose a moment earlier or the crazy leap to respond to my whistle that was to come seconds later.

I had wanted pictures to keep, to share, but I realised that to do so all I had to do was write about it, just as I am doing now. That is my gift, such as it is, and I thank God for it. I maybe had no picture, but I had instead the corner of a wonderful tapestry, changing and growing.

I ran like a madwoman through the crunching leaves playing hide and seek in the golden sunshine. I spent the rest of the afternoon stretching out the idyll until the children came home for their teas. It did occur to me that perhaps I should feel guilty about wasting so much time, but I squared it with myself. After all, this might be the last of autumn's lovely days. I had not wasted it. I had spent it like a saved-up sixpence on something sweet and frivolous.

But against such days of near-euphoria I had to set the visions of the same dog in mindless, yelping pursuit of someone else's ewe, running the terrified creature into a ditch and pulling great mouthfuls of wool, ignoring my desperate entreaties, deaf to me, blind to me, conscious only of the animal at her mercy and with a look in her eyes that disappeared as soon as I got near enough to touch her. But once that look had passed between us, I had lost her. And the trust that seemed possible on the sweet, sunny days with Rosalie in the wood was replaced with grim doubt that brought Ruby, too, to the point where she had to be confined in an outbuilding or fastened ignominiously to a length of rope so she could wander round the yard.

She was thus bound when Jim's 'Mac' found her, and their whole protracted copulation took place on the end of that old frayed rope. The final twenty minutes with Mac tied, his passion spent and his master whistling three fields away, his eyes betraying his agonising desire to be away, his organ's residual tumescence making flight impossible, were a tragic comedy that drew a hundred human parallels.

I was reminded of a story of Noel Coward – probably apocryphal. When a little god-daughter asked him 'What are those two doggies doing?' he is said to have replied that the first little doggie had gone suddenly blind and the other public-spirited doggie was pushing it all the way to St Dunstan's! In the case of Mac and Ruby, who somehow managed to end up back-to-back after exploring all the possibilities of the canine Kama Sutra one would have been hard put to it to guess what they were up to had one not observed the encounter from the outset.

But on that day there began one of the happiest chapters in a chequered narrative. Imagine, if you will, a cross between a wet hamster and a premature ferret. Something vaguely verminous, creeping across the damp kitchen floor like a dispossessed mole. Something so hopeless and forlorn that one might almost imagine it to be carrying all its unsavoury little possessions in a grubby carrier bag.

And there, in a smaller-than-average nutshell, you've got

Turpin. When Ruby fell victim to the charms of Jim's Mac from 'next door', I was secretly delighted. Even more so when two local farmers ordered pups before they were born. This was the first time we had ever had puppies of our own in the house, and I picked the brains of my dogbreeding friends, learning, as does the newcomer to any field, so much about the possible disasters attending such matters that I felt sure that the odds were piled so heavily against success that I should never have allowed the pregnancy to continue.

But they came, safe and sound, all black and white and defenceless like a quarter of liquorice allsorts, every one marked differently and every one a tiny treasure. There were six. In the first few weeks from the dropping of the litter to the appearance of their myopic navy blue eye-beads, it became obvious that five of the pups, all fat and sleek, were doing fine, but one of them seemed to shrink as the days went by. A prettily marked little dog with no tail at all. I bought milk substitute and helped him out with a tiny syringe, caring more for the little shrivelled thing than for the five fine siblings. In all my years of rearing animals of all kinds, I have found that the loving and caring is always fiercest where the need appears greatest. It is as if Nature and I were fighting for these hopeless ones. So often they slip away without putting up much of a fight, and one can easily convince oneself that it is 'for the best', but sometimes they pull through, by the skin of their teeth, and bring their own special joy. Like Turpin.

He was named at birth, because of the black highwayman's mask that distinguished his piggy little face. When I fed him I used to sing the old ballad 'O rare Turpin, hero . . .' and later he would blink his blank orphan-Annie eyes to the familiar sound.

His brother and sisters grew fat and mischievous, their eyes boot-button bright, ears akimbo, ready for any adventure; Turpin still appeared blind, a tiny creeping thing terrified by the sound of the sharp puppy barks that the others so soon developed. They picked on him unmercifully, singly and in a gang. He was often dragged across the floor by one leg, by the scruff of his neck, or even one tiny laid-back lug, by his hoodlum brethren. As I said to the children, it seemed probable that Turpin, if he ever grew up, would do so with a deepseated belief in divine providence. Whenever he was in trouble, which was often, his terrified squeals were answered by unseen hands which scooped him to safety, delivering retribution to the aggressors on the way.

Perhaps, I told myself, I shouldn't favour him so. But then again, he was clearly special. And I'd always had a secret place somewhere deep inside for underdogs and lost causes. On the other hand, perhaps it is a national characteristic. Charles Kingsley described the duty of an honest Englishman thus:

> Do the work that's nearest
> Though it's dull at whiles.
> Helping, when we meet them,
> Lame dogs over stiles.

There are worse ways to spend time.

Whenever I take photographs, there is always a period between the rolling-up of the exposed film and extracting it from the Brownie and the sending-off of it to the processors. This period varies in duration according to the state of the family exchequer. When we're fairly flush, I'll send off the films almost straight away, but when things are a bit tight there are always far more practical things to spend the money on, and so often I will find a roll of exposed film and send it off with no clear idea of what it might contain.

Only recently, back came eight pictures that summed up a lost, golden age. There was Taffy, the new boar pig, fast asleep with his pink stubby arms round Rosalie, clearly quite at home. There was the little heifer, Charity, up to her knobby knees in mud and still fuzzy with the winter coat that was coming out in handfuls. There was Ruby, the perfect mother, with her fine litter of gleaming pups. And there was Turpin.

One photograph in particular summed up all the hopelessness of this, the smallest of that litter of pups. Ruby, lying on the step in front of the door, with her children in a row, sucking happily. And Turpin, trying bravely to haul himself up the four inches of concrete that must have looked to him like the Old Man of Hoy.

Dear Turpin. He just didn't grow like the rest of the litter, and I fed him his special milk, little and often. Many were the nights he spent in the oven (on 200°F, with the door propped open!) and I was always surprised to see him alive in the morning. When I syringed his food into him the milk would come trickling back through his tiny nose, and I assumed that I had poured it down his windpipe and that he would die of pneumonia before the next feed fell due.

It soon became apparent that to leave him with the rest of the litter would be to sign his death warrant. The others would heave him out of the nest and he would be too blind and weak to crawl back. So I kept him, carrying him round in my pocket like an infant kangaroo, and prising open the tiny mouth every hour or so, forcing the milk oh so gently down the tiny gullet only to see it re-appear at the tiny nostrils and drip, drip, drip on the floor.

One of his first attempts at eating canned dog food was almost his last, when one of the firm and appetising lumps appeared to get stuck in his windpipe – and there began to grow a vague realisation that there was something more basically wrong with him than the inexplicable absence of tail in a breed where the tail is nearly half the dog. He was weird, hanging on to life for no better reason than that he seemed to know I wanted him to.

At eight weeks old he could not walk without stumbling. His eyes were beady-bright behind the black mask and his nose was wet – but the wetness was a perpetual snotty dribbling that did nothing to suggest good health. His breathing rattled and his whole appearance would have provided a visual definition of the word 'hang-dog'. Everything drooped.

At ten weeks, it was time to part with the puppies, who were becoming a serious expense. Two of his brothers and sisters I gave to neighbours. Three I sold to interested farmers at the livestock mart. But Turpin I took to the vet, shrivelled and snuffling, but too dearly loved to be given away and too precious to be sold.

I asked the vet to give him a check-up. If the poor tailless, sniffing thing would never be a healthy dog, then I would have him put down. But if there was the slightest hope he might thrive, he should get his routine inoculations and we would keep him – though for what, God only knew.

The vet did not mince his words. Turpin was a mess. His taillessness made him unbalanced. An overshot jaw gave him that perpetually soulful expression. His habit of trickling gravy from his nostrils after meals was due to a cleft palate and the gelatinous dewdrop that hung constantly on the tip of his snout was due to the irritation of that condition.

But would he live? Was it fair? So many people, on hearing my tales of his many disasters said that it would be 'kinder' or 'better' to put him down. I left it to the vet. He took his time over his answer, knowing that it was to be what I wanted to hear.

There was no doubt that Nature had made an awful lot of mistakes in this pup. She had tried to make good her oversights by letting the little chap fade quietly away, but I had interfered. With love, and with understanding of his problems, he would be all right. On the way home, I bought him a collar.

And eventually, he began to grow. Almost imperceptibly his legs lengthened and the skinny bird-feet spread into mighty paws. His white muzzle lengthened – at first just enough to make room for a scattering of black spots like currants in a pudding, then prodigiously until the upper jaw hung like a proboscis over the ridiculously short lower jaw, giving him an expression of perpetual resignation, while at his nostrils the familiar purulent exudate ebbed and flowed.

His black eye-patches parted in the middle to give his face an air of honest inquiry, and there appeared random patches of golden tan, one above each amber eye, like a pair of bumblebees, and others lining his hind legs and decorating the brave rosette where his tail should have been. His cranium rose to a point between ears that steadfastly refused to prick, and he began to show signs, not of canine intelligence, but of an uncanny understanding of what was going on around him and what contribution he might make to it all.

He was never apart from me – at first because it was not safe to leave him until he had mastered the art of eating without choking – and later because there was never a good enough reason to leave him behind. He travelled in the basket on the front of my pushbike, his ears streaming in the wind. He learned to hitchhike, travelling in any vehicle without complaint, so long as I travelled with him.

He gradually mastered the art of eating safely. He lies down with the bowl in his arms and throws his head back with every swallow. I have learned to adjust the consistency of his food so that it does not leak back down his nose. Only the occasional delicacies like rice pudding and custard bring on the cataclysmic sneezing fits that send great strings of canine bogies flying across the room, and for these he is forgiven.

One of my favourite memories of his adolescence is a sort of freeze-frame of one of his early efforts at helping with the sheep – standing eyeing the flock, his shoulders lower than his hips, one paw raised, utterly intent on the grazing sheep, while there hangs from the end of his nose a slim candle of grey-green snot, trembling gently in the breeze. There rose in me that day a great wave of aching love for this dear, imperfect creature, that was almost frightening as I realised how near I had come to the wilting, mincing, anthropomorphic sentimentality I had so deliberately avoided for so many years. And that I had found my dog at last.

My head is full of pictures. Turpin asleep, huge body folded on a chair, his head hanging down and his tongue gradually protruding, out of control, like a sliver of smoked salmon. Turpin lying before the fire listening to Beethoven, his legs bent like a crisp frog on the crown of some country road. Turpin singing, by request, head thrown back, mouth like an 'O', holding his part in the tenor duet from *The Pearlfishers*, with his skinny arms tight round my neck. Turpin far from home, waiting for me when I'm taken short, then solemnly pissing on the self-same spot, in the ultimate dog's compliment. Turpin guarding and caring for all that is part of his life – sheep, pigs, children; Turpin generously finding room in his great heart for all that is dear to me. Turpin trustworthy with the boldest ewe, the weakest kitten. Turpin on a walk in the dark, just the sound of toenails and a nose pushed into my hand. Turpin sharing the lost, bleak nights when despair comes too near, making himself close and still.

Turpin at my heels and in my heart.

One-horse Race or
a Chapter of Accidents

I enjoy a happy rapport with children, which I have always attributed partly to my having been one myself and partly to the ease with which I can call to mind exactly what it was like.

This being so, I should have been able to summon up a similar sort of affinity with ponies, having been one myself for a year or two. I was six, and re-starting my schooling after a nine-month absence in hospital and convalescence. That absence and the hugeness of the experiences that haunted it had created a chasm between me and my peers that I did not know how to cross. So I made no attempt to do so. Home was real, and the classroom almost so, but in the between-times, when I was alone with the other children who shrieked and darted like orchestrated bacteria in a pattern that I no longer understood, it was so apparent to me that I was not of the same species that I assumed the characteristics of another.

I can remember no conscious choice. I was a pony. A little grey pony. *The* Little Grey Pony, and spoke of myself in the third person, under my breath, recounting my autobiography as I galloped around and between the other children, who ignored me utterly. I had not yet come into contact with the niceties of horse-parlance and therefore I was not grey in name only, appearing defiantly white to all but the cognoscenti. I was grey like fag-ash and elephants, knowing no better.

I had a saddle. It was a flat, black shoulder bag, with a zip, and a sewn-on bright red 'A' made of some sort of plastic so that its points were sharp and comforting to picking fingers. My mother gave it to me to protect my underwear from all the chalk and Plasticine that assailed it as I resumed my school career.

For all those months in hospital, during which my few real possessions had dispersed with wear and tear and staff changes, had made me desperately possessive of anything I considered to be truly mine. While in hospital I had taken to swallowing anything of value in the belief – my knowledge of human biology being no greater than that of the average five-year-old – that these treasures would become part of me, and therefore inseparable. This has stood me in great stead; I can swallow pills, tablets or capsules by the handful without a qualm. My children marvel. But I have never told them of how I began with shoe buttons and graduated, on the Boxing Day of 1947 to a small, knitted doll, my share of a girl guides' charity parcel!

And now, back at school, I found I was being constantly asked to make, to create, all sorts of artefacts, which I was then supposed to set at naught, to hand in and forget, and I found I was unable to part with these small creations and even, at times, with the materials lent to me to make them.

So down the front of my vest, up the legs of my knickers, went drawings, patterns, cut-out figures and Plasticine animals, and also chalks, pencils, counting bricks and the odd component of the clumsy visual aids that were in vogue at the time. Mother gave me the bag and I stuffed it daily like a hamster-pouch, but, at playtimes, when I was cast out among the whirling dervishes, I would slip both arms through the strap, which would then cut comfortingly into the back of my neck, while the bag itself bounced against my buttocks as I raced round and round, narrating my adventures as I ran.

On the face of it, this should have formed the basis of some sort of understanding of the workings of the little Shetland pony I took on as part of the picture of rural self-sufficiency I was trying to create around us. In the event it proved as much use as a bicycle to a goldfish.

Perhaps Magnus was a particularly sensitive pony. Perhaps he believed he was something else. Perhaps I am not one of those to whom affinity with the horse is natural. Perhaps he really was the intractable little demon he often appeared to be. But since he is no longer with us, perhaps I should give him the benefit of the doubt and shoulder the blame for an experiment that was based on blind faith in a preconceived idea of the qualities of horseflesh that sat as uncomfortably on the square black shoulders of that petulant palfrey as I did.

Maurice Cox, in his book on the Shetland pony, states that they have 'tremendous character, marvellous memories and show more sense and intelligence than other breeds'. Other people, real and self-fancied horsepersons alike, asserted that the fault lay in my failure to dominate him. I, in my innocence, believed that the desire to serve would be the natural reaction on his part to affection and loyalty on mine.

When it came to serious training of the little rogue, I enlisted first of all the aid of a young lady who was known locally as a fine horsewoman and someone with a natural understanding of animals.

I was starting at the very beginning. I have catalogued in *Faint Heart Never Kissed a Pig* my early difficulties with the horse literature available to me, now I was faced with the niceties of mouthing, lungeing and long reining, which last was, so far as I then knew, something incumbent upon the monarch as expressed in the national anthem.

I put Magnus and myself entirely in the hands of this young woman, who arrived at the first appointed hour mounted on a horse called Shadowfax, who inspired confidence, and accompanied by a neurotic dalmatian, who dispelled it. I went to find Magnus and we led him into a small, flat field near the house.

I put on him the makeshift bridle with the mouthing-bit he had been wearing for a few hours each day, like a child getting the feel of a wire brace to straighten its teeth. 'Lish attached the clothesline, took my long hazel switch, and began to send him round, first at a walk, then at a trot, apparently responding to the words of command. I had a go, at first dreadfully self-conscious, most afraid of showing myself up in front of my young adviser. But I warmed to it as I began to feel the sense of circus, the beginnings of affinity with the creature.

This would, perhaps, be more likely to lead to some sort of working relationship with Magnus than my original vague ideas of training him with encouragement and gentleness, or of riding him cross-country to a standstill, like they do in the cowboy movies, and which always results in a lifelong rapport between man and animal.

The second time 'Lish came, we took the bridle and the rein and a bucket of flaked maize. I caught him, and he came with us like a horse-on-wheels for a little way, then suddenly reared and plunged, dragging 'Lish for maybe fifty yards before she was forced to let go and he disappeared into a spinney. He was caught again with the flaked maize bucket – a victim of his own greed, and subjected to another lesson. I reflected that Magnus' mother spent most of her life in the household of the Duchess of Devonshire. Could this have affected his attitude?

The third time 'Lish came we went down the fields to look for him. He stood among the alders by the river, watching. Then, when he deemed we had come close enough, he whirled like a picture-book pony and galloped off, his fat buttocks juddering with every footfall. 'Lish smiled. 'There,' she said, with every evidence of satisfaction. 'That

shows he knows who's going to boss him.' 'So it does,' I
said.

But I had to make some sort of effort to turn Magnus into
an asset rather than a liability, albeit an attractive one. I had
to justify him firstly to myself and then to so many people
who had begun to look to me as some sort of rural guru. One
of the dangers of writing a column that takes the form of a
diary is the temptation to deviate from the paths of strict
honesty in the attempt to build up an image of oneself more
in keeping with one's daydreams than with actual reality.
When I adopted Magnus I saw myself riding round the
countryside, driving smartly into the village, hauling peats
from the moor and carrying everything everywhere in style.
It was only a matter, so I told myself and everybody else, of
teaching the pony. As things have turned out, what I was
able to teach him was but a drop in the ocean compared to
what he taught me.

It was one Easter Monday a year or so ago that I learned
that it is possible to muck out with your feet. Not a
momentous conclusion, you may be thinking, but it was the
best answer I could come up with for the doctor at the
Friarage Hospital who had told me on the Friday that I must
not do the job with my hands. It would never have done for
the Foreign Legion, but it meant that I could clean the floor
of Magnus' yard so that he could wear his mouthing bit for
an hour or two in safety without access to the wisps of straw
and hay that wrap themselves round the keys and might
choke him.

Mind you, as I set my feet firmly at ten to two and did a
marathon Silly Walk round and round till I had gathered a
neat pile of FYM roughly in the centre, I did fall to thinking
that it might have been simpler just to choke the little fiend
with my bare hands. Or rather, my bare hand.

We had set off, the children and I, with Magnus, to collect
a few potatoes for lunch. I held the lead rein while Caroline,
a young visitor, steadied him from the other side and

we gentled and persuaded him to walk quite presentably through a fairish stream of holiday traffic. All good practice. He was doing well. The only minor incident was the slipping of four wellies and an equal number of hooves on the loose grit left over from the February snows, but we had all regained our composure by the time we reached the bottom of the hill, and when the other children caught up with us, we clattered in fine style up to the farm where we hoped to get the spuds.

Two bags loaded and hung on to the trace-hooks that I had mounted on his saddle, and we were away. Two cars passed us without incident and we were going steadily, if slowly, back down the road. A vehicle appeared behind us. Then another. Since this was Magnus's first load of any size, I didn't want to hurry him. I indicated to the leading vehicle that we would pull into the layby about 20 yards ahead and the driver and his passenger smiled. We pulled in and the car sailed smoothly past; I think I let go the lead rein with my right hand for a moment, looping it loosely round my left, to acknowledge the courtesy of the occupants. I know I smiled, because the smile was still frozen on my face a split second later when the driver of the following vehicle drew to a stop beside us, wound down his window and told us where he thought we should have been, then whisked off with a swish of air brakes.

Magnus reared, jumped up the bank above the layby, dragging Caroline with him and leaving his load behind. I found myself lying full-length but with the knot at the end of the lead rein grasped firmly in my right hand. I felt pleased that I had not let go and that the pony was still under control and I reached forward with my left hand to take in some of the slack. It was then that I noticed that the top of my third finger was no longer where I had left it. It leaned perilously sideways and there was a nub of bone sticking out that I had certainly not seen before.

The look on Caroline's face showed that she realised what

had happened, and she raced back to the house where we had bought the potatoes to fetch help. Patched up and stitched together, I was forced to admit that the only part of the proceedings that was hard to bear was the sight of the record card which told the world that I had been brought to such a pass by a Shetland pony – it was like confessing to having been run over by a pram.

I left Casualty with a finger like a sterilised sausage and suffered severe pain during that first night which diminished gradually to a vague nuisance. I was left with an uncomfortable and ridiculously inconvenient splint which held the finger rigid to avoid my being left with a digit crooked forever in a constant come-hither. I learnt a hundred new skills as a result.

I rediscovered all the things that can be done with nose and elbows that the mother of twins learns during their first 12 months. I found a whole new technique for straightforward knitting. I reconstructed my early method of typing and developed a neat way of fending off the billy-goat while I bottle-fed his daughter, that involved sitting on his neck and poking the bottle between his horns.

I perfected the simple act of handwashing, which is surprisingly difficult when you're used to having another hand to wash it with, and milking was a doddle, it just took twice as long, like everything else.

The only thing that really galled me was that, after having gone through all that for a load of potatoes, I was quite unable to peel them.

It is always so easy to give the novice in any field a heap of good advice, but the very fact that he is a novice often prevents him from putting it into practice. It is always more satisfactory to show than to tell, but people just don't have the time nowadays to do that.

A great many of the people round here once had horses working for them and were prepared to tell me a lot, but none had time to show me. Even in the advice there was conflict. You can't drive a horse, said one, until you can ride it. Another maintained that no horse could be safely ridden until you could drive it. Both experts. Both right, somehow, I supposed, but all the time Magnus got older, content to come when called and to be led like a seaside donkey and all the time I knew in my heart that as each month went by a good, sound little pony was being sadly wasted.

Ever the optimist, I bought a cart, ridiculously over-priced, and a complete set of harness for which, at the time, I had little use. The man who delivered it was part of a large and extraordinary family who more or less have the monopoly of the scrap and small livestock business in and around Northallerton. Not quite gypsies, not yet tinkers, yet having about them the air of both. I liked them and told them just how far I'd progressed with Magnus's training.

A week later, they came back, with a ramshackle trailer behind their spluttering car, loaded the pony into it, had the cart upside-down on the dented roof, and drove away, promising miracles. A month later, Magnus was back. He trundled into the yard, hauling the pretty blue and yellow flat cart that had seemed until so recently a useless acquisition and looking every inch – all forty-two of them – a carthorse. He had left us looking like a neglected, over-stuffed settee and now he shone with health and vigour. I was delighted.

Delighted not only for us because we now had the mak-ings of a working pony, but for Magnus himself, who deserved better than to be messed around by a bunch of amateurs, however well-meaning. The people who taught him regaled me with some hair-raising stories about their early efforts and I laughed, but I knew deep down that I couldn't have coped with a horse that stalled on a level crossing or insisted on executing an elaborate quadrille each time he encountered a drain.

They showed me how to harness him. It was easy when I'd been shown, but when I read about it in books I almost wept with frustration. I got John Seymour's book on practical self-sufficiency, but even that assumes a degree of prior knowledge that I had not yet aspired to. It's all very well telling someone to be sure to fasten the dooberry to the whatsit, leaving room for the thingummy but they assume you can identify these things on sight. I needed an exploded diagram, like an aircraft kit, and couldn't find one. A pile of harness is a depressing sight to the uninitiated. It holds about as much promise as a plateful of spaghetti until you know what you're doing. It doesn't take a genius to work out that the blinkers go on the front end, but after that I confess I was all at sea.

But now I could do it; I began to talk knowledgeably about breechings and cruppers with the best of them, and when we set off up the hill to fetch the feedstuffs down and the yellow wooden wheels trundled on their iron tyres and my young passengers were shaken so that their voices wobbled and they got the giggles, I dare swear that no experienced driver of a four-in-hand got more of a thrill. The road looked new and exciting when seen between two black ears and our confidence in traffic grew.

All the same, we did add one thing to the cart before we set off – 'L' plates.

I am sure you'll have heard at some time or other the expression 'Hold your horses!' I often use it myself. Sometimes a child would come home from school with a new idea, news of an outing or the latest playground gossip and as one word tumbled over the next in its anxiety to reach me, I would often halt the chatterer with a quick hug and the admonition 'Hold your horses'.

Or sometimes, when being given a lift and struggling into a strange safety-belt, I have asked the driver to hold his horses, just for a moment, until I got settled. All my life, I think, I have bandied the phrase about without paying much attention to it. I know my mother uses it, and her father often used to say it when I was in danger of rushing headlong into anything. 'Hold your horses.'

It was not until I met the new, schooled Magnus that I fathomed what was meant by that remark in the heyday of the horse, when the holding of them was something one paid small boys to do outside public houses. When I started driving Magnus in his cart I was made aware of all sorts of hazards to which I'd never given a great deal of thought. One of these was his extreme reluctance to undertake any outward journey. Another was his enormous enthusiasm on homeward journeys. I discovered that he associated the feeling of added weight on the cart with the signal to set off to such a degree that, having felt the one, he did not wait to hear the other. I'm told it's a dreadful fault in a horse.

Anyway, I reminded myself of Pavlov's dogs and forgave him temporarily, though resolving to cure this somehow. Pavlov, in case you don't recall, made the great discovery that if you ring a bell before feeding dogs, they get so used to the idea that their mouths water when the bell rings, regardless of whether food comes or not, thus cutting out the middleman, as it were.

Now Magnus, being a bright little pony, became used to the commands 'Whoa – stand!' and obeyed them grudgingly. However, he also became used to the feeling of my weight shaking the cart slightly which preceded my command to 'Walk On'. And if I wasn't careful, and didn't make it up to my driving seat at the first leap, he was inclined to set smartly off and I had to make an undignified scurry and a snatch at the reins. Most of the time I was ready for him; but we did have an accident that taught me a salutary lesson.

All the neighbouring cattle were gathered round the little hut where the delivery driver left the pig meal and I took no notice. After all, they were Magnus's best friends. It was only when I put the meal-bags onto the cart that they showed any interest at all. I think they thought the cart was a new kind of trough and I was feeding them in it. They all surged forward, and Magnus chose that moment to waddle

forward with the cart. It was only a step or two, but as I
called him to a halt again the cart wheel touched the leg of a
Limousin calf and he kicked out, hard, catching Magnus on
the leg. Magnus fled, cart and all, into the next field and the
cows and calves galloped after him, bellowing and kicking
out with their knobbly legs. It was chaos.

There was no question of holding my horse. He ran, and
there was nothing I could do about it. Oh, I ran too, because
it seemed better than nothing but I might as well have been
standing still. Away he went, the cart rolling crazily from
side to side, every timber screeching, adding to the pony's
panic. I was somehow seeing the whole thing from behind
and above, and I was reminded of the wagons and stage-
coaches in the great Western movies; I seemed called upon to
pull off some kind of stunt, to do something – anything.

But I was left far behind as Magnus swerved off the road,
through the trees that edged it, miraculously avoiding the
snatching branches, and thundered straight down the field
towards home. I saw him jump down on to the road again at
the bottom. I saw the cart jump after him, reeling sideways
like a stricken ship, landing somehow on its iron wheels and
when I panted up behind, Magnus was standing by the gate,
waiting for someone to open it.

I knew that what I should do now was drive him up the
road again. But I could already feel as though it were
happening, the strain or urging him through the gate, the
tenseness in my whole body as he steeled himself then
spurted over the drainage offset on the crest of the hill, and
the very real fear as to what might happen when we got to
the gate at the top. And I didn't bother. I unharnessed him
and let him go. And I knew in my heart that it was never,
ever going to work. And that slightly less than half the fault
lay with the pony.

High up on top of the hill the cattle munched their way
through the spilled pig meal and a hush descended on the
day.

There were other days, and other accidents. One of these, when Magnus took fright at a tractor, resulted in the cart and pony all but changing places and left me lying in a ditch alongside Magnus, who was sitting up like Eeyore, totally unable to rise without his entanglement causing further panic. I had to wait for rescue, and still recall being extricated by the gamekeeper, who unharnessed Magnus under my instruction, and how the nonchalant use of all the correct terms for the various bits of leather did nothing to comfort me in my confusion.

Clearly we had to consider parting before we killed each other.

One day a man called to buy a billy goat from me, and saw Magnus and his cart. His attempts to persuade me to sell left me so overawed that he mistook my silence for refusal and upped his already enormous offer. I said yes.

The time had come, I decided, to take the first step into the twentieth century. I had been preparing the annual account for the smallholding and had come upon a huge nest of bills relating to transport. Ferrying kids here and there costs phenomenally, and simple things like ferrying me when I've got more food than two arms can carry was becoming a major household expense. I'd had a good offer for Magnus, complete with all his carts and harness and, having decided to take it, I bought myself a motor cycle.

The decision wasn't taken without a lot of thought. I was totally convinced that it was a good and practical idea for Magnus as well as for us or I wouldn't have entertained it. I still think so, in theory. And so I started on a whole new chapter in my life. A motorised mother. A candidate for membership of Hell's Grannies, joining at last in the full camaraderie of the road, as it were.

The bike was delivered rather late on an evening in August. It was almost dark, and too late for a test flight, but as the dew began to fall, I somehow manhandled the new acquisition into the back kitchen, propped it up on its stand

and found out what all the knobs and things were for. I consulted the little Japanese manual that went with it and wrote a précis of the starting procedure on a little sticky label and fixed it carefully inside the legshield. I trimmed the new L-plates to fit and fitted the new tax disc into position. All licensed and insured, I was ready for the road.

Not the real road, of course, but the long tarmac approach road to the house, with its steep hill and sharp bend, would be a marvellous practice track until I felt ready to cope with the Queen's highway.

First thing in the morning, there I was, crash helmet fixed on and gate opened ready, quivering with exhaustion from manhandling the bike out of the back kitchen again, which was somehow ten times more difficult than getting it in, and standing tentatively astride my little bike, lifting my leg from time to time like an enuretic puppy and stamping my foot on the kickstart pedal to no effect whatsoever.

I felt cheated. I had copied the instructions faithfully from the manual, but, like most manuals, it preached but briefly and only to the converted. 'Open throttle slightly' – but what was slight? I'd never had it started so couldn't tell. 'If cold', but was an engine still cold when someone had been kicking at it for half an hour? I remembered dimly something about people flooding things if the choke had been out for a long time, but did this apply to me?

In the end, deeply humiliated, I had to go and ask George if he would show me how to start it, and he hopped into his Landrover and came round, while I pedalled behind on my pushbike, feeling small. He showed me that in the case of this particular bike, opening the throttle slightly meant exactly half way, and that, in the case of people less than five foot three tall, bikes are more easily kickstarted from alongside rather than astride. Simple when you know how.

I turned the bike round so that it was facing the gate, then started it. I eased it off the centre stand and put it into first gear. I opened the throttle as gently as could be, but I still seemed to leap forward like an over-eager kangaroo. I put on the brakes and everything stopped. Most reassuring.

I let off the brakes and moved again, but I had not realised that the brakes and the front suspension were in any way related, and when the bike seemed to move upward rather than forward, I imagined that I was about to do a mighty wheelie, for which I was not ready. I grabbed for the handlebars because that's where I was used to finding brakes, and found, as any motorcyclist would expect, only the front brake; at the same time I tried to put my foot down, thereby altering the direction of travel, and at the same time yet again, I opened up the throttle with a hoodlum sort of roar and did a wheelie-for-real, right up the rockery and over the edge.

Both the bike and I landed back on the road, but not in quite the same place, or exactly at the same time. I righted the machine, got back on, and drove in fits and starts up the hill, but my chest ached because I didn't dare breathe till I got to the top. I had dented the wheelrim and my confidence, but I had made it to the top of the hill. As a matter of record, I parked the bike there, walked down again, had two cheese toasties and a cup of tea, and then went up again and rode it down.

I realised, with a dull misery, that these were exactly the same negative sensations with which I had come to approach a journey with Magnus, and the familiarity of the feelings brought a rush of regret.

Within ten days I had crashed the motorbike.

I didn't think it possible for a middle-aged mum, pulling away in first gear from a standing start, to deform the front end of a motorcycle so severely whilst leaving the mini with which we had come into contact with nothing worse than the loss of a bit of trim from its wheel arch! It was a silly accident – a caravette had pulled in and was flashing his lights in an irritated sort of way for me to hurry across a cattle grid, and while I was making my L-plated way laboriously out from the place I'd pulled into to do the same to him, the mini overtook him and suddenly, to my inexperienced eyes, appeared to fill the road. I over-reacted and locked my front wheel, sailing merrily into the mini while steering wildly in the other direction. As I lay in the road apologising to the driver of the mini I knew that it was all up with the poor bike.

I was just returning, too, from my first journey of any length on it. I had explored the full potential of the gearbox for the first time. I had practised emergency stops on an empty road and felt for the very first time that I was beginning to like motorcycling. Even though I had never exceeded thirty miles an hour, I had felt the thrill of swooping round a bend and down one hill and up another, using throttle, gears and my own body to make the motion magic. And now I was worse off than before; reduced to hitchhiking again, but with knees that no longer bent as they should which took all the pleasure out of walking. Oh, I was fully insured of course, but not against the worst part of all – the pitiless coverage afforded by the local CB network.

The only consolation I could find was that, had it been my poor Magnus and not the motorcycle lying on top of me in the road, things would have been much worse.

I was sorry for the motorbike. It deserved better. But at least I didn't have to shoot it.

The Other Business

'When did you start writing?' and 'Where do you get your ideas?' are the two questions most often asked of me. The second is unanswerable – except by such tart rejoinders as 'If I knew that, I'd go there' – but the first is something which I have often asked myself.

Writing happened, like reading and I'm not quite sure how either came about.

I remember my first day at school, summoned to the desk of Mrs Morrison, a tall Australian lady with a row of large teeth which rose above a gathering of spit-bubbles like tombstones thrusting through mist, who referred to the boys' toilets as 'the gulley'.

'Mummy tells me you can read' – and I felt betrayed. I couldn't read – everyone said that was why I had to come to this place. Mum had never suggested that I could read. What would happen when Mrs Morrison found out? Would I be punished?

She put a little buff-coloured card in front of me: 'What does that say?'

I remember the blunted corners, the crude illustration, the very type-face 'Mother see Kitty. Kitty can play ball. I can play ball, too. See me play ball with Kitty.'

'You can read very well,' said Mrs Morrison. 'Good girl.' And I learned my first lesson at school. That reading and telling an adult 'what it said' were one and the same thing.

I have always supposed that writing came into my life the same way, but what I called it when we first met I can't remember. I am sure, though, that my first attempt at the definitive modern novel did not take place until I was at least eleven!

But over the years, as the children have grown up, and the holding progressed from a foundation through an enterprise to a business, writing has emerged as the only constant, the spar to which I have clung throughout life's tempest, as it were. I grinned as I wrote that: just because something is true doesn't mean it may not also be ludicrous, after all.

It sometimes worries me to think that if we didn't live in such a remote place, if we were on a housing estate somewhere within range of the social services, we'd like as not have been classed as a problem family when the kids were younger. Their clothes were often crumpled and speckled with cat hairs and their shoes seldom shone. We never seemed to have in our house the things that other families take for granted, like eggboxes, cornflake packets and aluminium foil, which primary school teachers expected mothers to produce at the drop of a hat as essentials for craftwork.

Later on, cookery lessons were a nightmare because we never seemed to have any sugar that wasn't in the tabletop jar, all damp and sprinkled with coffee dregs, and we usually had to pick marmalade out of the measured amounts of margarine.

On one thing, though, I insisted. That was a proper respect for our language and the finer points of its grammar. I let them get away with throwing used teabags at one another, and making houses with the furniture, but clipped their ears for saying 'different to' and taught them how to tell when to say 'Johnny and me' and when 'Johnny and I', rather than how to tie their laces.

I have always looked upon gratuitous swearing as a sign of

impoverished vocabulary, and although no words are taboo in our house, the children were brought up to appreciate that some words cause offence in some circles and that they should choose with care.

There are some words that we don't use in front of Grandma-the-noo, as we call my Scottish mother-in-law, not because the words themselves are bad, but because it would upset her to hear them and when there is a choice of courses of action, we do the kinder thing. One four-letter word, though, we all use. It refers to the heaps, lumps, dollops and piles that our livestock leave behind them. I see nothing wrong with that – it's just a word, and much older than the prejudice against it. I remember once Nancy used it in conversation in front of friends and their mother snapped tartly that Sammy and Susie (the names have been changed to protect the innocent) had been brought up to refer to it as 'poo'. I found that word offensive and asked the children not to use it in front of me.

So why do I let Turpin out and tell him to go and lay eggs, when on the face of it it is as tacky a euphemism as poos or whoopsies? It was just the first thing that came to my mind as I groped for a substitute when I realised that the other word sounded so much like 'sit' that it was confusing the poor little pup who was being trained to do one of those things on command and the other on a sheet of newspaper.

And in the interests of the continuity of his education, I stuck to it. It is proving as difficult to outgrow as the Initial Teaching Alphabet. But it works, after a fashion. This, of course, leaves us with the problem of what to call the fine buff-coloured fruits of our busy hens. Would you believe, cackleberries?

Only words after all – and that's what I write, for such as the Prince of Denmark to read – words, words, words. As far back as I can remember.

One Saturday, I hitch-hiked down to Osmotherley to post a letter. I missed the collection, but met up with an old acquaintance in the village hall. Once a month, a sale of second-hand books is held in the village, proceeds in aid of the church fabric fund. I go when I can, but always a little diffidently, because I know that one day it will happen. One day I will go into the hall and there, on one of the trestle tables, will be a copy of one of my books. What will I do? It is a personal nightmare of mine; my own room 101. I have had indications of how it will be. Chastening experiences they were, too, as are all intimations of mortality.

Some time ago I rescued from the Oxfam shop a battered copy of *Argosy*, the last of the great short-story magazines. Nobody knew, as I paid my penny and stuffed it in my bag, that it contained the first of my own published stories. A little piece of my own life.

And only last month I went to a grand farm open day nearby, where all the doubtful delights of modern agri-business were on display. There I discovered a new and sobering use of newsprint – shredded up by the metric tonne and spread out under the feet of housed cattle, to absorb more bullshit than we journalists had put into it in the first place.

There I stood in the village hall, looking out of the corner of my eye at the main table, while I selected some more volumes for my poetry collection from the bookcase in the corner. Shelley – Catullus – Eliot, and when I was sure it was safe, I turned my attention to the rest of the books. And there, right in the middle, was a novel by William Sansom.

Sansom. My hero. A gentle influence and an occasional encouragement to a young writer he had been good enough to notice. He was a master of the short story, bringing to each one a perfect balance of craftsmanship and fun. He always maintained that he didn't enjoy writing novels, likening the work to the keeping of a boarding-house. I picked up *The Face of Innocence*, lost in memories.

Sansom believed that the chief problem with fiction was not content, but style: 'How to put it freshly; how to freshen up your prose yet keep it classically acceptable.' He said the best way to do it was to 'read a few pages of good stuff'. How often it was to his stuff that I turned for inspiration. Another thing he believed was that there was a need in literature to find magic in what are called 'ordinary' things. This belief I share. I still remember how delighted I was when one of my stories was published in an anthology along with one of his, and my name appeared in the montage on the cover, sandwiched between Sansom and Eric Linklater.

I still have a letter from the editor of *Argosy*, passing on some most flattering comments from this fine writer. It ended with the words '. . . so you see, you really mustn't disappoint both Sansom and me.' I recalled his kindness across twenty years and my grip tightened on the book. I hoped I hadn't.

A man stood beside me. 'That's one of the ones the wife brought across,' he said, looking at the book in my hand. 'Have you read it?' I asked him. 'Oh, yes,' said he. 'Did you enjoy it?' I asked him. 'I don't remember books once I've read them,' said he. And I was struck by a strange mixture of sadness and irony – and drama too. There were precedents for this situation. I was holding in my hand the earthly remains of a truly great influence on my youth, and in his honour I must speak!

I held out the book, deliberately, at arm's length. I laid my hand on the man's shoulder in a gesture that was pure Gielgud. And I said:'Now get you to my lady's chamber and tell her, let her write books a foot thick, to this favour she must come; make her laugh at that!' And in the place where writers go when they have exhausted this world's potential, Sansom laughed. I heard him.

Now in those high and far-off times, when I was a junior sub in Farringdon Street, a by-line column was the height of my aspirations – but it can be a humbling thing now that I hold it in my hand. I have substance, you see, only on

Tuesday nights. The rest of the week I am but as pocket-fluff and damp Kleenex.

To be here today and gone tomorrow, that I could bear with equanimity but, as things are, on Tuesday nights I am part of the media-scene, but then instead of disappearing with dignity, I become part of the environment – stained with salt and vinegar and blowing in the gutter outside the chippie; my face staring up from the bottoms of a thousand budgie-cages and my rural philosophy and barbed wit cut up into random squares and hung in khasies all over the circulation area.

Had we but world enough, and time, this smallness, Lady, were no crime . . . In Marvell's original poem, of course, he berates his Lady for coyness, not smallness, but the former has never been a particular problem of mine, while the latter has been causing me, of late, all sorts of difficulties.

I decided, in the interests of better grassland management, to divide our only bit of decent pasture in half. I had a spare sheep-net, and a load of rather superior stakes that someone had given me for firewood. I laid the stakes out, made holes for them with the cow's tethering-pin, then set them up and made ready to drive them home. I found that the wretched things stood taller than I did, and when I lifted the 14lb hammer on the four-foot shaft, I fell over backwards, literally, in my efforts to hit the stakes. I had to go back home for a rabbit-cage to stand on.

Then I tried to help my neighbour Jim to take down stones to fill up holes in one of his meadows. He let me drive the giant tractor to and from the rubble-heap, and it was as I was on my way down with the first load, approaching the gaping hole at a rate of knots, that I found there was not enough of me to apply enough pressure to the brake and clutch pedals to make any impression on the beast's progress. I had to fling myself forward across the instrument panel with my arms round the steering wheel, pushing down on the pedals with all my might.

These things all served to confirm in me the ever-growing realisation that I lack stature. The idea dawned during one half-term, when Andy and a group of his friends got together to discuss the 'A'-level General Studies paper they had just completed. I was drawn into the discussion.

'Read that, mum,' said Andy. 'It should interest you.'

And so it should, I thought miserably. It was a weighty piece about politics and the media, and dealt with things like journalistic intrusion and the role of the Press Council and the IBA. I felt shamed and small. To be a member of what I like to look upon as one of the caring professions and to be so lackadaisical in my attention to its more serious aspects is, perhaps, a great waste of opportunities for tub-thumping and axe-grinding. Who really knows where I stand on nuclear disarmament, feminist issues or European economic policy?

I touch lightly on them all from time to time, but what light, in the words of a question in Paper I, do I throw upon the human condition? I lack stature. That General Studies exam paper worried me! I was able to impress all the youngsters by my confidence in the multiple choice questions – but then that sort of general knowledge comes easier with middle age.

Long after the kids were back at school, turning their attentions to the physics and biology papers, I was still debating the ways in which journalists might be 'confronted with their failings and shamed into improvement'. The trouble was, the only concrete things I'd been ashamed of during the previous few weeks were a split infinitive or two and a sentence which guttered to a conclusion without a main clause. And nobody seems to mention the journalist's duty to be literate.

I thought about some of the other questions – one in particular ' "We know more than our ancestors did but there is no evidence that we are wiser, more moral or more creative than them." Discuss . . . how far you think this statement can be justified.' There can surely be no justification whatsoever for grammar like that!

There are times, though, when the writing of others is of paramount importance.

This is by way of being a tale of two Saturdays. A somewhat Dickensian look, if you like, at the best of times – and the worst of times. Everyone has bad days, but the first of those two Saturdays was the worst I'd had for a long time. An accumulation of all sorts of problems, with one major one looming so large that I couldn't see round it. Oh, nothing new; nothing I hadn't faced before, but a sleepless night of unashamed self-pity had left me bleary-eyed and weak, and I cycled half-heartedly into the village for a few groceries, wondering where, apart from that, I was going.

When I was a kid, my head was full of romantic notions of what it would be like to be a writer. Starving in a garret was part of it, I recall, la vie bohème being an important part of creativity. As a young adult, city bred, I resolved to remain true to my vision of a simpler, gentler way of life. What I hadn't prepared myself for was the responsibility that comes with heading a family, the sheer weight of the dependence of a stock farm, however small.

I met the postman. A great, bluff whirlwind of a man, driving the scarlet Landrover as though he were delivering Milk Tray to Miss World, yet always managing to make his delivery two hours later than any other postman on our round. He always has something to say. He quotes from postcards. He holds out letters he knows are expected as thoughtless people hold out biscuits to dogs, snatching them back at the last minute, to make them drool and beg.

One day I shall bite him.

That day, though, he handed me a small brown envelope. 'No big cheques for you today,' he said. I took it and fled, freewheeling down one bank to get as far as possible before I had to get off and push the bike up the next one.

A small, brown typewritten envelope. Inside, a typewritten letter. From someone I'd never met. Joyce Fussey, a
funny, happy lady whose work I have read and enjoyed. She
embarked, as I did, on this hill-farming treadmill, at about
the same time. She had written to me, out of the blue, a long,
loving and very personal letter, one small part of which I will
share with you. 'I just wanted you to feel that somebody
understands what you are doing and why you are doing it,
and hope things will become easier for you . . .'

I had put the bike down at the side of the road; now I
got down beside it and cried. Not, I feel sure, the reaction
that Mrs Fussey had envisaged, but she wouldn't have
minded if she'd known how much good it did me. And then
I picked up the bits and got ready to start again.

During the following week, things sorted themselves out,
as things have a habit of doing, and the next Saturday, I
started again for the village trading post, singing at the top of
my voice. I met the postman again – this time it was the
fresh-faced young man who always apologises for being
later than half past nine, and never forgets to change the
'next collection' flag on the postbox. He handed me another
letter, and again I lay down on the bank to read it.

This time it was an hilarious letter from Michael Clegg,
the naturalist, well known to all local country lovers. A
wonderful stop-go, telegram-style letter that crammed in
a great wealth of news and fun, peppered with his own
personal word-cartoons. His little Bedlington terrier being
forcibly ejected from a pub named after that distinguished
breed. A querulous magpie, much puzzled by an unrecog-
nisable portion of his breakfast. I leant back in the grass, and
said aloud: 'You great, daft bugger!' then went on my way,
laughing.

Only a week between two Saturdays. And two letters,
bringing home to me how fragile is this self-sufficiency and
how precious, despite the veneer, is the touch of others.
Two letters. But to me they were so much more. A squeeze

of the hand from Joyce; a slap on the back and a 'now then how are you?' from Michael. Bless them both.

It is undoubtedly a privilege to correspond regularly with a whole city and I am often conscious of how easily it might be abused – or at the very least used for my own personal ends. Looked at from another angle, though, it furnishes me with a means of giving, through expression of things that have been felt sometimes by almost everyone, sometimes by just one or two people, who then reach out to me, and their touch is precious.

And sometimes I am able to offer my status, such as it is, to the people around me. I have never put more care into a piece of work than went into the obituary for my neigbours' handicapped daughter. It was my gift to them of this slight talent that so often distances us from each other. I would have given more than I dare confess to be sure that they understood this.

Only once did any circumstance prevent me from writing my regular contribution and it was a grief that blotted out everything for a while. And when I returned to it, it was to accept it for what it was. Not a sideline, but a need. A part of myself. It seemed a long time since I wrote the column that had become so much a part of my life. And, funnily enough, it was almost difficult to start again; it was as if I were taking up the threads of our life after years away from it, instead of just a week or two.

When I came to put a fresh piece of paper into the typewriter to tell all that had been happening since I last wrote, I had to take out the beginning of an article I was writing on the eve of the Summer Games, describing the joy with which we awaited the visit of my brother, Kevin, an annual event which had become one of the most joyous festivals in our calendar.

I had told of his last visit, when his special present to me had been a handful of little plastic penguins, which he poured into my hand like diamonds, and of the laughter when I told him how dearly I had always wanted just such a present. I told, too, of how his hitch-hiking made the times of his arrivals unpredictable, so that one minute he would be expected and the next he would be there, his great arms bear-hugging us all at once and straight away belonging as though he had never been away.

I never finished that column. Kevin was killed on his way up to us and we shall not see him any more. Identifying the body of a loved one is a great help towards accepting the fact of their death but it does not take away the anguish of remembering daily, hourly, that they are no longer alive. Somehow that isn't the same thing at all.

The blessed escape into the heavy, repetitive work of haytime was a cushion against the sharp edges of misery, and time and time again I sat at the typewriter, determined to tell of the loss, the unhappiness, as if somehow I could share it and at the same time write it all away.

I wanted to write an obituary for Kevin that would be so perfect, so complete, that when people had read it they would have known him and mourned him with me. Time and time again I took out half-finished pages and tore them up. They were cheap somehow, satisfying neither the need for consolation nor the longing to recreate the astonishing young man I had known and loved for all of his 25 years.

I smiled and quipped at his funeral, playing at being strong, and pushed to the back of my mind the futility of it all, the emptiness, the overwhelming incredibility of his not being there. I returned to search for him in the quiet places he needed, now and then, to visit, and in the summer tasks he loved to share.

I had been lucky, I realised, to reach this age without having to face the death of someone for whose going I was unprepared; someone I was not ready to live without. For weeks I believed, as I know all of us must believe at such times, that my own grief was something hitherto unexperienced, that there had never been a greater loss. Grief at least explains an arrogance it cannot justify. And time, while it can never heal such scars entirely, can move them gently backwards until at least the whole thing can be seen at once, in a kind of quiet perspective. I loved him; but he is gone.

One night I awoke to a great thunderstorm. Lightning that stayed all round in a constant flickering glare like faulty neon and thunder that cracked with a terrible proximity as though it brushed my face through the heavy curtain of loud rain that ran, quite warm, down my bare legs and into my wellingtons as I fought my way through it to the gutter behind the house, where the ducklings cried for help, floundering against the brown swirling current that threatened to take them into the dark cavern below the old dairy.

I threw them, one by one, over the half-door into the barn, and all but one were saved. Then I got a sack and began to rescue the young chickens, whose brave little mother stood in the floodwater brooding the only three of her precious fourteen that her tiny frame would still accommodate. All of these went squeaking into a sack and were tipped out into the safety of the pig-sty. It was only then that I realised just how many of the things I should have been doing as routine had been thrown aside or left undone because of my monumental self-pity. I was ashamed.

I went up the hill at the back of the house to the place where I planted a eucalyptus tree that was given to me in remembrance of Kevin by someone who never knew him but understood a great deal. The deluge had not harmed it and I was relieved.

I had determined to put some kind of tiny memorial on the rails by the tree; something so original and perfect that it would say everything there is to say about loving and losing – if only my tired brain would show me what to write. But in that moment of quiet after the wildness of the storm, I knew what it must be. Not a new thought, but something two thousand years old, written by a young man whose brother's death had caused him great grief. He caught that moment I had just found and held it for ever – the realisation of his constant presence; the acceptance of his eternal absence . . .

Atque in perpetuum, frater, Ave atque Vale.
Hail and Farewell.

When I write, I reach out with something in my hand, offering. Like a child hiding behind an armchair, passing notes to the family. Sometimes it is the only way I can bear to tell the truth. Sometimes it is the only way I can laugh at myself in comfort. Sometimes I long to make a final distinction between the two, like ruling off one piece of work from another in an exercise book. And sometimes it doesn't matter.

Can anyone tell me why it is that the people in whose hands I have to place myself now and then in the furtherance of my literary career, as it were, are getting younger by the minute?

For a few days I had the design manager of a firm of paperback publishers staying at the house, creeping purposefully through my daily routine with a couple of cameras dripping with special lenses and more knobs and levers than one would believe possible. And he was so very young.

From my earliest days, I have been warned about policemen. I was taught to look out for that special landmark – the day when the uniformed officers begin to appear young and vulnerable, and so carefully have I been watching our dear village constable for signs of regression into a second adolescence, that I was caught unawares by the schoolteachers.

I went to a parents' meeting at the local comprehensive and, since it was after hours and the kids were out of uniform, I really couldn't be sure which were the staff.

Having come to terms, though, with this one minor

discomfort, I found the whole thing most enjoyable. I suppose it is different if you're a real celebrity and photographers could be almost anywhere and often are, but I didn't really have time to get bored or irritated before young Mark was on his way back to London and everything settled into its normal pattern again, like a bowl of custard when you take out just one spoonful.

I was a bit alarmed to discover he'd taken 120 pictures when I had been aware of only a couple of dozen, but it's too late to worry about that now. And anyway, they couldn't all have been like the sweet, romantic scene of the milking of the family cow.

Now that Charity had calved, you see, she had to be milked from time to time, and since we are both novices in the field, there have been one or two occasions when things have not gone quite according to the textbooks, and the occasional contretemps has resulted in wet feet, an empty bucket and dried milk in the tea.

All the same, it's not as risky a procedure as it was at the outset, and when I was asked if we could turn the morning milking into a photocall, I was happy to oblige. It went well. I achieved a healthy bucketful of 'gold top', and took it into the house to cool, then came back and took my seat on the stool for a second attempt. (Having harvested a goodly quantity of clean milk, I always nip indoors to make it safe before finishing the job, a bird in the bucket being worth two in the bush, as it were.)

I returned to where Charity was tied to the drainpipe outside the back door and carried on milking. 'Could you look this way a moment?' asked the photographer. Charity heard him. As I turned to smile at him, every inch the country gentlewoman, she brought up her nearside back foot and planted it firmly in the bucket, pushing downwards with all her not inconsiderable might.

But we had a good laugh about it, and the little pigs enjoyed clearing up the spillage.

We wandered down and had a word with Jim, who was turning hay. Mark got a few shots of the tractor and we turned to go. 'Bring us down the greasegun when you have a moment,' asked Jim, and when we got back to the house I picked it up from the wall where he'd left it.

Mark took it from me. 'I'll take it down,' he said. 'My legs are younger than yours,' and I smiled ruefully to myself and planned a brisk jog to the telephone box before lunch. That would show him. But he was a very nice young man, and no touble at all. I looked after him as best I could. I felt I owed it to his mother.

Can anyone tell me why it is that the people who help to shape my life are getting younger by the minute? On second thoughts, don't bother, I think I know.

But paddling in the little waves that frill the edges of celebrity can have its farcical side, which inhibits one to some extent from plunging in whole-heartedly. I was in a state between panic and euphoria. I was due to speak at a Yorkshire Post Literary Dinner next day and I was sitting at home in the old striped shirt that serves me as a nightie, writing my column, in an attempt to take my mind off the event for a little while. I had only just recovered from appearing as a guest on an afternoon chat show to publicise my last book, and was pondering the somewhat ambivalent status of a person who appears on a commercial television programme which has no commercial break in it. Think about it!

Other, famous authors were due to speak, and while in some ways that was a comfort – after all, the guests would get value for money even if I didn't burn myself upon their consciousness like pokerwork on a wooden tray, so to speak – in other ways it was a terrifying thought. They were, after all, the main attraction; I was very much the supporting programme: I could almost hear them saying 'Ann who?'

Behind me, the room looked like a jumble sale. I had been trying to find something to wear, and all the ideas I had looked so horribly odd when I tried them on that I was feeling thoroughly demoralised. I had tried on every shirt, blouse, T-shirt and top that I possessed, and none of them looked right. I was perfectly aware that the best of them was a sort of lurex tube I got in the Oxfam shop because it was just what I was looking for, but it was so horribly itchy that I was not sure I could face sitting in it for any length of time. Common sense told me that I could not deliver a speech while clawing at my armpits like a flea-ridden gibbon; but that narrowed the choice down to the cotton lace-up top I wear for sheep-clipping, and a thermal vest, which, in the end, I wore.

I had no idea how I was going to get there. I could not get in touch with anyone who might know. I decided I would ask the local taximan to come and run me to the station. I had thought of stuffing all my finery into a carrier bag and hitch-hiking, but I was expected, they said, at a sherry reception at a quarter to seven, and you could not tell that to a lorry driver on the A1 without sounding a bit gauche.

It was bizarre, too, how life went on despite the impending occasion. The lambs still had to be fed, and Diana, the pet piglet, still wiped her filthy little snout down my trousers whenever I let her out. It is hard to feel like a celebrity when holding an earnest conversation with a fat, pink pig.

I was sure the other authors would have real lives of their own which they would have to leave at the door when they entered the hotel, but none of them, I dared swear, as socially unacceptable as mine.

I felt something of a traitor to it, though, when I remembered that I had bought a huge bottle of bubble bath so that I could wash it off before I went and would feel even worse if I had to sneak out without hugging the dog, so as not to get hairs all over me. But somebody still had to muck out the pigs. And so long as they still loved me, and at least one reader still loved me, I felt sure I would take the dinner in my stride.

I decided to go outside, to practise my speech on Diana . . . pearls before swine as it were.

In the Front Line

One of the dangers of writing about animals on a regular basis is the barrage of labels waiting to attach themselves to someone whose reactions to recurring situations are fairly predictable. I am adopted by like-minded people as a mouthpiece for causes that I do not necessarily espouse and sometimes I am quite seriously worried by the pigeonholes into which I am thrust by readers who will take a thought, an idea, an ephemeral reaction to a situation that I am still exploring, and trap me with it, like shutting a genie in a bottle or a spider in a jamjar. And then I am shelved and labelled, protesting my innocence or ignorance or both. I am becoming surer of my feelings on many of these subjects, but I am not ready to lead a crusade.

It is not hard to write about animals. It takes a kind of courage to write about writing about animals.

It was spring. I sat on a tuft of gnarled old ling a little way up the moor. Far away both to right and left the heather-burners were out and there were ribbons of flame shaken out across the hills. The old stone wall at my back was warm from gentle sunshine. I found it hard to concentrate in the house on such a rare fine day, and the possibility of passing visitors sent me in search of solitude in one of the outdoor studies which had been too cold for use since the last fine days of autumn.

I still sometimes need a day like that to remind me, once in a while, of why I came to live here, and of the deep, sweet pleasure in simply being myself and in harmony with my chosen surroundings. Far over the moor the TV transmitter mast reached up to poke a rude finger through the only cloud in a wedgwood sky and the distant purring of tractors marked the re-awakening of the land, helped by a gentle shake from a ploughshare or two. There was soil under my own fingernails because I had been digging – not so much for victory as for survival, and already I seemed to taste those first early peas and smell the bitterness of the earth on newly pulled baby carrots. The urgency of the season was upon me.

Sitting there in the heather, it was strange to reflect that for years after I arrived in the Dale, people were saying that it was unlikely that I, a Londoner, would stay long. They seemed sure that I would find the comparison unfavourable and head sooner or later in search of bright lights and traffic jams. I was faced with amused tolerance rather than outright prejudice, but I can never expect to be looked upon as a local by anyone other than more recent arrivals than myself.

But then, why should I? It is as senseless as the current chafing for equality of opportunity to expect to become, as it were, naturalised automatically, simply by virtue of having settled in a spot of my own choosing. It is the choice itself that is the most important thing. I am here because I want to be. I have seen and shared life on the other side of the hill, and have chosen this, for myself and the children, and although I still admit to a private personal grief for the loss of my special city, I am now as proud and possessive about this Dale as any of those with a more obvious right to such feelings.

Those are the feelings that took a shaking-up when the hunt came. From a distance, it seemed terrifyingly without pattern, this gathering of dogs and scattering of people, with the unpredictable rushes of one or the other in any direction.

I felt angry and uneasy and there was no pleasure in it at all, even though I was trying my hardest to feel something positive, something favourable, in deference to many of my neighbours with whom, on this one subject, I am totally at variance. I am an anti.

In a neighbour's house some time ago, one of the keenest followers of fox hunting I know rounded on me and said that I was one of the people who said that fox hunting was cruel, and I was rendered speechless by the remark, because this is something I have never said. Even when I watched the dogs streaming down the fields across the river, heard the horn echoing down the valley, I don't think it crossed my mind that there was a fox involved at all.

If I push him to the forefront of my consciousness, I suppose I do think it a rather barbaric way of controlling pests, but then I have poisoned rats and eaten rabbits and justified that to myself, so I cannot claim to be against the actual killing. No, it is the hunt itself, more than the hunting, that upsets me. Who gave these people the right to career, willy-nilly, through other people's livestock, rush headlong over other people's property and provoke, for the time they are within sight and earshot, a sense of unease, of threat, in all the things whose paths they cross?

In all the recurrent publicity about the effects of strange dogs on ewes prior to lambing I've seen no clause exempting fox-hounds. Last year the hounds, on that occasion entirely without human support of any kind, came through the fields above the river at breakneck speed. When they entered one small field, it contained an old Masham ewe heavy in lamb, and when I next passed it, it contained a grief-stricken old Masham and a dead lamb. Had it been a picnicking family whose dog had been seen in that field, the case would have been considered proven.

When I opted for country life, I accepted the rules and have honestly tried to the best of my ability to keep them, so that until I became a friend to my neighbours I might not be a nuisance to them. I would never allow myself the measure of arrogance necessary to set aside those rules in pursuit of my own pleasure, and I resent other people's doing so.

I can imagine what it must feel like, riding at speed over the countryside, but there are well-known ways of ensuring that the route taken is that of least discomfort and inconvenience to others, and I cannot believe that the enjoyment would be so much less simply because the fox himself has to be overlooked in favour of a more predicatable quarry.

After all, sheep being kept in inside fields at this time of year are presumably in lamb, and cattle have no early warning system to lessen the shock of being scattered by a pack of howling dogs. People who hunt care about horses – what if those horses were scattered and terrified by a pack of hooligans on motorcycles, who rode round and round their paddock oblivious to the creatures' panic?

The person who invented the phrase 'to ride roughshod over . . .' was perhaps standing as I was in the middle of a field in the centre of a little knot of frightened animals who felt threatened by the presence of so much sudden strangeness in their usually placid pastures, and perhaps felt the same surge of anger at the intrusion. I believe that every person has a right to pursue his own interests insofar as they do not conflict directly with another's. When such conflict occurs, compromise must be sought. Compromise in this case would seem to consist of a fair warning, such as is given, with cheerful goodwill, by the organisers of the occasional motor car rallies in the area.

Obviously, no clear idea of a route can be given by a group of people committed to following the course dictated by a hunted animal which may be discovered at any point and may head in any direction. So the fox himself could surely be excused attendance for the common good, and a course laid that would be variable within reasonable limits. This would, as a side-effect, increase the pleasure of attendant spectators, if this is of any interest to the hunting fraternity.

As things stand, the hunting folk are the Hell's Angels of the countryside, and I resent their intrusion. I am an anti.

How badly people compare with animals sometimes. I am often accused of misanthropy because I claim to prefer the company of animals when I have the choice; I often do, though the reasons are very much my own. But one or two pictures have made themselves important in the formation of an attitude which worries me whenever I confess to it, and if I quote them perhaps I can justify in some measure this claim which, taken at face value, presents me as a sentimental freak.

A trip to the zoo. A caravette full of excited children. And a couple of small billy goats hugged in little arms. We were on our way to present these little goats to the local zoo in return for a free day for as many children as we could get in our vehicle. A friend drove us down in her caravette and we all felt we were getting our money's worth.

One of the problems of goat-keeping is the disposal or destruction of the surplus billy kids, who come whether they are wanted or not. I found one of the happier ways of solving the problem was to give them to the zoo, who kept them as pets in the children's corner until the zoo closed for the winter, when they were put down and used to feed the large cats. This seemed as sensible an end as any and I argued my conflicting principles into a state of truce and tried hard to enjoy the day out with the children.

But children in a zoo are hard things to enjoy. I can see them now – children who visited my house regularly, children I liked; children I loved – behaving in a manner so hateful I have remembered it with devastating clarity ever since.

An orang-utan. Looking old, but then they all do. Not doing a lot. Just sitting, reawakening all my old feelings

about zoos – and then a little boy, leaping in front of the cage
and landing legs bent, in front of the poor captive ape. The
child's arms swung loose, a little distant from his body,
he crouched lower, thrusting his buttocks backwards, con-
torted his face, straining like a baby trying to fill its knickers,
grunting with effort and satisfaction. Then he began jump-
ing up and down on flat feet, grunting, menacing, roaring,
shrieking, thumping his chest with his clenched fists; then
his sister, a lovely, golden-haired child I thought I knew,
joined him in the hideous game. And I held tight to the hand
of the nearest of my own children. She looked up at me and I
saw with gratitude my own horror mirrored on her face. For
her sake I yelled at the others to stop, and I was told some
home truths by their parents. I was over-reacting. And the
orang blinked his sad little eyes and didn't react at all.

It was early in the morning when I left home to slip along to
the telephone box, but I went by the road all the same,
hoping for a lift. An estate car rumbled up behind me and I
smiled and thumbed, but the elderly couple inside looked
surprised and a bit frightened and the gentleman's foot
leaned a little more heavily on the accelerator as he pre-
tended not to see me.

It was in the sudden silence that the big car left behind that
I heard the faint cry of a baby bird. It seemed to come from
the middle of the road, but I was sure my ears must be
deceiving me as no baby bird in its right mind would be out
in the open in broad daylight.

I looked carefully all around and there he was, right on the
crown of the road. I went cautiously up to him. It was a little
pheasant. His instinct from the moment he was hatched
would tell him to run and hide at the first hint of danger,
returning only to the safety of his mother's breast when all
was peace again.

But he stood quite still in the middle of the road and his
cheeps grew to a frenzied staccato as I picked him up. Then I

realised why he had not run away. He was completely blind. Both his eyes were glued shut with congealed blood and his baby down was stiff and spiky. He smelt of death, yet he appeared uninjured. I held him and listened. There was the sound of another chick nearby.

I could hear the tiny, tentative mouse-squeak at irregular intervals that keeps threatened chicks in touch with one another without betraying their whereabouts to anybody but the most careful listener. I found this one, though, without much trouble. All the skin was peeled from the top of his little round skull and his stumpy wings were held tight to the sides of his body. I put him and his brother down the front of my shirt where the warmth and darkness would keep them quiet while I listened for others.

It was as I reached down to pick up another little lost baby that I saw a hen pheasant crouched in the grass. She was flattened and puffed out in the manner of all female birds brooding young. I had been as near as this to sitting pheasant before and I was sure she would fly as soon as I made a move.

I wondered if I could put the three little lost babies with her, even if they were not hers and I made a grab to hold her still while I fished down the front of my shirt for the chicks.

I needn't have bothered. She was quite dead. Cold and stiff. Then, as if from the dead bird herself, came a faint cry. I turned her upside down and there were little blood-stained feet, pedalling wildly under the feathers of her stiffened wing. Four more baby pheasants were stuck in the mess of black blood that had flowed from the neat round holes in the breast beneath.

I didn't bother with my telephone call. I took it all home – the body with its adherent casualties and the three survivors inside my shirt, and together the children and I worked to free the other unfortunate chicks.

We didn't save them. Only three lived long enough to try the foster-warmth of the old broody hen who spread herself to accommodate them, and they weren't strong enough to survive the ordeal. We made a small hole and buried them all together.

Someone must have had a reason for shooting her out of Season. I wished I understood. It's just that it all seemed such a terrible waste, and somehow I wanted to acknowledge her passing.

I can appreciate that a violent end to a non-predatory creature is not contrary to the laws of nature, whereas the slaughterhouse, battery cage and the sow stall undoubtedly are. But is man by nature a predator? And if he has a choice in the matter, which way should he exercise it? And if a sow could carry a hod of bricks, would she build herself a stall? I am not sure; I can only see the pictures.

Last New Year's Eve I went for a walk. I went further than usual, to places I'd not yet discovered, with Turpin trotting alongside. We were looking for Rocky, our Swaledale tup, who had gone astray. I'd decided that it was time for him to come down from the moor and stay in the fields, but he didn't agree and jumped out on to the road and headed for the hills.

But not our own hills, unfortunately. He went in search of talent somewhere on a neighbouring stretch of moor, or possibly among the fields and woods of another estate, and I'd been searching for him.

Not the sorrowing, desperate search for a lamb, lost and alone, or a pregnant ewe who might be in trouble, but the leisurely, happy hunting of a fit young sheep who can take care of himself. He had been sighted once or twice, but Turpin and I had not yet caught up with him.

New Year's Eve was windy and wild and there was a promise of rain in the air. There was excitement, too. I enjoyed seeking out the small, sheltered places on a strange, new moor, and the old enchantments of space and freedom reached out to me in a way I thought I had forgotten, so that I ran like a child around each new corner and chatted to

Turpin about what we found just as I had done to my imaginary dog when I was a little prisoner in a London garden.

But it was Turpin who found the fox. We were following a fence above a plantation of larches and he bounded ahead. I saw him stop, and heard a sharp bark, and when I called him he came to heel at once, but licked my hand and galloped forward again. I was on the point of calling him back when I saw it too – the lithe red-gold form of a fox pressed tightly against the wire.

Instead of admonishing Turpin as I had intended, I called urgently, afraid for him if he faced a cornered adversary. I ran to him, he ran to me; the fox did not move. I approached it cautiously at first, then ran forward with a cry of anger and pity at what I saw.

It was a vixen, the rough wind making creamy swirls in her new winter coat. She had slipped out of the wood through a small hole in the wire fence, in a desperate bid for freedom, but around her body, above the hips, was a glistening snare that ran back to a rotted wooden stake, too large to slip through the hole behind her. Who knows how far she had come from the place the snare was set? Who could guess at what she must have suffered, and for how long?

Her lips twitched in a halfhearted threat. Here now had come her two greatest fears, mankind and his dog-servant, and she made a feeble effort at defiance. I laid down the long crook in my hand, wishing it were a gun, and knelt by her. At first, I tried to slip my woollen glove over her snout, because I was afraid of her teeth, but it seemed too cruel to fill her nostrils now with the scent that she had been taught to shun from a cub. Her black lip pulled back again in a token snarl, and I saw that one of her canine teeth had been broken off at the gum by her futile efforts to chew off the snare. I imagined one of my own teeth broken, each breath drawing cold air over the exposed nerves, and I felt my skin crawl.

I turned my attention to the snare. Perhaps even now there was hope. I talked quietly to the poor creature as she lay in my lap to take the strain off the wire. Turpin laid a huge white paw on her, sniffing encouragingly, and I felt the thrill of terror run through her and sent him further away. I remembered the game we played as kids, winding elastic bands round our fingers, and seeing how long we could wait before releasing them, savouring the pain as the circulation returned to their stiff, swollen tips, and I could feel it again.

And somewhere in those few moments, she died. It was not something that happened to her; more something she did for herself, as a last resort, an escape from pain and the fear of my presence in her helplessness. She summoned all her pride and courage, and opened the last door to freedom. And I cried. For her. For what had happened; for what we had done. For Man's arrogance and cruelty. And for my own.

Turpin gave me his puzzled look and I rose to go, feeling the comfort in his strength and simplicity. He seemed to be asking about the vixen, and why she wasn't coming with us. I shook my head. 'Too late,' I told him. Too late.

Not long after we came to the Dale, I discovered that I had a supreme talent for trapping moles. And I destroyed many hundreds –not because I had any reason of my own, nor even for money, although Jim paid me the princely sum of a shilling for each little body, but because it gave me a special status. It was a genuine country skill that I had found by accident and I was determined to make the most of it. But I couldn't hush my conscience for long. Even when I carefully skinned each mole and pinned out the little squares of velvet on the old privy door, I could not convince myself that these deaths were justified. And so I did not do it any more. There just wasn't a good enough reason.

And with this thought, another of the local customs, to

my mind more honoured in the breach than the observance, slips into focus.

Turpin's training as a sheepdog was progressing reasonably well. I'm afraid he's never going to be one of those black lightning-streaks that you see on television, responding like a highly-tuned machine to a single shrill whistle. Partly because he is too soft and gentle, and partly because I have never been able to whistle to save my life! Oh, I can make a passable tweet now and then, and even, when temperatures and humidity conditions are just right, follow through the odd tune, but when it comes to a life-or-death situation and a whistle may be all that stands between me and some major disaster, like my dog driving the sheep in the wrong direction or flying into the middle of a group of penned sheep and sending them like a starburst, scattering in all directions, then the inner surface of my mouth shrivels like a prune and my lips go all slack and refuse to purse, and I stand dumbstruck, quite unable to avert the inevitable, as it were.

But Turpin is going to be, God willing, the sort of dog I really need, who comes round the sheep with me like a third leg, never in the way and only participating in the proceedings when asked to do so in plain words.

I need a dog that will let me sneak about among the sheep, getting a good look at what's there. Recently I lost one. One of the previous year's lambs – a hogg – still wearing her wool. The weather had gone cool, the hazelnuts were ripening, and it was too late to clip her, even if I found her, but all the same, Turpin and I went up and wandered whenever we had the time, enjoying each other's company. The sheep clipped earlier were growing their wool again, and the bigger lambs were beginning to look more like small adults, and the issue became more confused every day, but I never gave up hope. This young sheep of mine had been seen, by me and several neighbours, skipping cheekily off from the rest with a few of Jim's hoggs during a drive, and she and they had dodged all the gathering dogs and men since then.

It was time for the local farmers to begin to make their way to the arable farms further down-country to bale up the straw behind the combines and bring it back by the trailer-load to feed and bed their livestock in winter. They were too busy for shepherding for a while and for those few weeks the moor seemed to belong to me and Turpin.

And it had changed over those weeks. The bracken had achieved its amazing annual maximum, so high overhead that it took courage to plunge into its sweaty, fly-ridden depths to flush out the sheep. And the heather had changed from the awkward, bristly green covering the moor had worn so long, to a carpet of picture-postcard purple; not the purple you can give a name to but the soft, singing-sweet purple that comes every year from deep in the memory of the moor itself, warm in the sun and throbbing with bees. Turpin and I flung ourselves full length in its transient beauty, and we were covered with a film of soft pollen, as though we had fallen asleep for years and woken in a pall of dust.

If only I could have taken you there, shown you the colour and let you feel the gentle warmth of the first autumn sunshine and let you breathe that wonderful smell. Oh God, the smell of that heather!

Turpin's ears pricked and he looked up, expectantly. I sat up, too. Sheep were moving, uneasy. Two or three broke and ran, almost stumbling over us where we lay. I heard a tractor. I stood up and watched as a column of men filed towards us, with fat bounding spaniels and white flags. I stayed until the first of them came up to me and asked, 'Training the pup?' in a friendly way. 'I was,' I replied, 'but we're going home now. We won't be in your way.' And I turned to go. The man said he wouldn't be long, that they were going to move off in a minute, he and the rest of the grousebeaters. He seemed a pleasant chap.

But we didn't stay. We went back home. And in the chill silence between the departure of the beaters and the first of the guns, I took one last sniff at the heather. But it didn't smell quite the same any more.

Winter's Tales

There were three things that brought about my decision to defrost the fridge. First of all, with the Christmas holiday imminent, I had gathered in a bit extra in the way of perishables and I thought it would be nice to put them all in a fresh, clean place. Secondly, there wouldn't be a lot of time for attending to such things when the holiday was under way, and thirdly, the excrescence of ice under the freezing compartment had reached such proportions that I couldn't shut the door securely and the cats could open it, thus defeating the main object of the subject.

I switched off and unplugged the fridge, spreading newspapers round it, and propping the door open before I went to bed. In the morning the lump under the freezing compartment was unaltered, the newspapers were bone dry and the inside of the window was encrusted with crazy patterns.

I resigned myself to the fact that it would not be possible to defrost the fridge until the temperature in the kitchen could be brought above freezing and went for some sticks to light the fire. Soon I had a merry blaze. I called Nancy to get up and ventured outside.

It was bitterly cold. Everything was iced. Old Snuff was covered with a solid crust and Charity had gone; in her place stood a magic creature all made of frosted tinsel. Every hair of her dense winter fuzz was silvered for half its length and her generous whiskers were sharp with ice. The dewdrops in her nostrils twinkled as the steady breath-clouds stirred them, and only the gentle brown eyes linked her with our lost friend.

Rosalie Pig ran out to greet me and found her trotters quite inadequate to cope with the sheet of ice that covered the yard. Over she went with a great resounding slap like a wet hand on a baby's bottom.

Turpin came out with me as black as ever and returned from his first madcap circuit of the yard grizzled with frost as though he had been away for years. Gloved hands stuck to icy rails and water froze in the buckets between the standpipe and the pigsty.

I had to let the goats out for a drink at the stream and found them remarkably easy to put back inside again, they had apparently no desire to stay out in such weather; even the prospect of mischief seeming less attractive than the warmth of their own house. I knew exactly how they felt.

It wasn't long before I scuttled into the kitchen to wrap my hands around a steaming mug of tea and peep out of the trickling windows at a world so changed and inhospitable that it did not tempt me as it usually does and I waited in the rocking chair for conscience to send me forth again. Our rocking chair isn't one of the sort that lends comfort to the old age of portly people on patios. It's one of those fat 1930s kind that squeeze backwards and forwards over a central spring and this particular one is utterly useless, so that it is most inadvisable to attempt to rock in it, or even to wobble with anything approaching abandon, as the slightest tilt aft sends the whole issue right over backwards.

I have become quite expert at balancing the thing. I really believe that the occasional tensing of the buttocks necessary to preserve that balance is vaguely beneficial in counteracting the droop of the Drysdale derrière. Nonetheless, on occasions my attention wanders or one of the cats leaps on to the back of the chair, upsetting the delicate balance of posterior power and over I go.

I bought it at a farm sale for 20p because there was a copy of Galvayne's *The Horse* among a pile of odds and ends under the cushion, and I sit in it as a kind of penance when I know I should really be doing something else. But after a second mug of tea, I knew I could no longer delay my daily walk up the moor to see the sheep. Donning oversized duffle coat and balaclava, I stumped forth in leaden wellies, a truss of hay under one arm, faithful hound at heel, and my breath puffing ahead of me all the way up the hill.

So many winters have come and gone since we began our sojourn in this strange and special place, and one of the questions I am most often asked is whether they are 'bad' or 'difficult', whether we are 'cut off' from the rest of the world, as though it is only in winter that problems arise. It is not ice and snow that has cut us off, so much as lack of transport, lack of cash, and very often lack of sufficient motivation, not only on our part.

The long winter of 1979 tested my resolve, but even that was not an unmitigated disaster, and after its mighty meteorological onslaught, succeeding winters have left a series of small pictures, like an embroidered border to the one, great landscape – one little snow, for instance, that came and went, managing a fairly orderly withdrawal, all things considered.

Even so most of it managed to pass by our house on its way to wherever snow goes. It was quite an impressive sight as it tumbled over the rough surface of the yard on its way downhill, provided you pushed to the back of your mind the fact that water is supposed to run underneath the yard through a nine-inch drain that was laid especially for the purpose.

I remember vividly the laying of that drain. A great yellow mechanical digger grabbing great gobfuls of soil and stones from a deep, businesslike trench on whose upper lip perched two toddlers, utterly fascinated by the procedure.

Those toddlers are now teenagers and when questioned, they denied having left anything around that might have blocked the drain. I suspected the ducks, counting carefully to make sure that none of them had been sucked down the pipe by the thaw's sudden surge. When I found them all present at evening roll-call, I borrowed a set of drain rods and groped at extended arm's length until, with two rods to spare, I encountered the obstruction.

With all the little tools in turn screwed to the end of the leading rod, I shoved, twiddled, picked and rammed. No go.

The consensus of neighbourhood opinion suggested that the drain should be opened above the site of the blockage, the tile below removed, cleaned, replaced, and the hole back-filled and made good in the best traditions of British civil engineering. Simple.

As I told you, the drain was originally dug by mechanical means. It was not a question of removing turf and digging nice healthy spadefuls of good, soft soil. The pipe lay below several feet of solid, rammed hardcore – broken tarmac, limestone lumps and battered brick, the whole made interesting by the presence of the occasional massive boulder. I borrowed a pick and began.

The first job was to divert the great rush of water so that it wouldn't fill the hole as I dug it. The answer to that problem was to cut a trench to lead the water off at an angle and use the lifted sods to guide it all where I wanted it to go.

When the actual excavation was embarked upon the enterprise nearly foundered on square one, because as I swung the pick aloft for a flying start the metal head quivered and then, as the shaft paused for a moment at the vertical, it dropped from top to bottom like that clock-thing at Greenwich, doing violence to my knuckles. I borrowed a crowbar instead.

Each prised piece was lifted by hand and laid aside, until the first of the biggies came to light. After a few tentative pokes with the crowbar it became apparent that the whole hole, as it were, would have to be enlarged around it. The spade was useless because the huge stone impeded its movement, so I fetched a cement trowel and excavated archaeologically until the boulder stood proud of the surrounding soil and was ready for lifting. I finally rolled it to one side to expose the drainpipe. Broken, it appeared by the weight of that great boulder.

There was the plastic boat that Andrew bought on his first school trip to Whitby. He wept so at its loss that I promised to open the drain, then wrote in secret to the manager of Woolworths at Whitby, who sent another in a plain wrapper by return, bless him. There too was the red plastic sandcastle bucket into which I milked my first goat, and a Mothercare baby powder shaker which brought back mixed memories. Now the water was thundering along below me, clearing out any remaining debris, and I watched it for a long time, wondering.

The weather is one of the recurring topics of conversation among hill farmers, perhaps with more justification than in some quarters. Even so, I sometimes get a little sick of it and long for an earthquake or a hurricane, to vary the topic at least of Sandra's meteorological monotony. From the end of August Sandra, one of my gloomier neighbours, brings up the subject of snow at every opportunity.

I made a particular note in my diary that she told me on the 23rd of October that she had seen on television that there was to be snow on the hills. I assumed that she must have dozed off in her chair and awoken to a documentary on a polar exploration or one of those old films where Ronald Coleman underwent some personal catharsis in Tibet. All the same I pulled aside the bedroom curtain on the 24th with a slight thrill of expectation which, according to my diary, was entirely without foundation as I appear to have spent the day picking potatoes.

Snow is cold, wet, obstructive and telltale, but it is still difficult to suppress that thrill at the thought of it, especially on a fine, clear autumn day when the pheasants' wings clatter overhead like a shower of newly minted pennies and the old carthouse is full of logs and peat and hay in readiness for its coming.

Since my early childhood, when my father, with a long journey ahead of him, threatened me with actual bodily harm if I were heard to use the phrase 'lovely snow', I have felt guilty about the childish pleasure the prospect evokes, and I remind myself intermittently of chilblains, soaked clothes, blocked roads and empty cupboards as a kind of atonement for my heretical attitude.

Gone at last are the days when the local people kept telling me that I had never experienced a really bad winter. I have shared with them what is universally acknowledged to have been the worst – and survived! Until the mighty snows of 1979, I felt that I had not fully shared in the heritage of my chosen home.

So many of my memories of snow are happy ones. To a lonely child in a London back garden, snow was like a holiday – a change of scene as uplifting as a Riviera cruise. The flawless crispness of it, spread like royal icing over the patchy lawn. The crystalline perfection of it tinselling the wrought-iron balustrade beside the stone steps which bore the imprint of a single set of small wellingtons going forth into the unknown, metamorphosed from the too-familiar.

Rushing under the sagging rose-arches to explore among the mysterious raspberry canes. Sleuthing on the tracks of tomtits and tomcats. Climbing the back fence to survey the frozen waste that was until yesterday only a neglected tennis court, and planning afresh the thousand sweet revenges of a child growing up alone.

There I am later in the family photograph album, building a prince among snowmen for the little brother and sister in whose eyes, at that time, I could do no wrong. Clearing the pavement outside our house, and extending the area by degrees until I overlapped my neighbours' gateways, thus earning an honest shilling.

Gawking off to grammar school, gymslip and felt hat, through a living advent calendar that had once been only a rather down-at-heel street.

These snowtimes far outweigh the bad, the frightening days, and even they, if I may permit myself the luxury of complete honesty, were stimulating, different, even fun – the way air raids and firewatching were fun for my parents.

I know that when the wind comes straight across from the house of my snowfearing neighbour, it is almost impossible to climb the hill against the flying spikelets of ice. That it freezes my face into a torment of exquisite pain, that feet ache and fingers nip. But simply to look at the hoarfrost on the trees is a generous measure of compensation.

If we get another winter like 1979, I may feel differently. I am not foolish enough to ignore the dangers to livestock, health and property, but if I were not prepared to face them, would I not have stayed in the city? If the worst comes, I will be able to take one step nearer the people around me, standing alongside them to help ensure as far as possible the safety of our livestock and of each other, for one of the brief periods of closeness I cherish.

Recently I called briefly at the house of my snow-Cassandra. She told me again that the weather forecast had mentioned wintry showers on the hills. One came. I watched it whirling down the moor to envelop me while I was out with neighbours gathering sheep. I turned up my collar; the dog flattened his ears – and then it subsided into a windtossed rainshower that washed the few flakes into the muddy puddles of the day before. The sad thing is that poor Sandra missed it, because she was indoors, watching television.

After one positively pig-sickening half-term holiday, I prepared to acknowledge that, blow the winter wind as it might, it wasn't half so unkind as man's ingratitude. But, personal troubles notwithstanding, the weather over that particular few days was extraordinary in its severity, and far be it from me to belittle its impact.

It had been a time for swapping stories of frozen pipes and icy escapades and for comparing chilblains in collective misery. I managed to get to the shops during the week, but nobody could negotiate the drive down to the house so I left lots of things in the henhut at the top until I could manage to carry them down. Even the pony and cart could not get through drifts like those, and so I trudged like a middle-aged yoyo, up and down, up and down.

The last trip fetched home, among other things, a couple of pounds of Cox's Orange Pippins. I tipped them into the fruit basket on the table without a second thought.

Next morning, getting up early to write my regular article, I grabbed one absent-mindedly and bit into it. I could make no impression and did a sort of silent-film double-take, believing I'd picked up something else by mistake – a bed-knob, perhaps, or something left in the night by a brass monkey. But no; it was a pippin as ever was – and frozen solid.

All day those apples sat by the stove but their icy flesh didn't yield until evening, when I stewed the lot of them and served them up with hot rice pudding for tea. At least the weather let up long enough to let the boys get back to school, but it was quiet without them.

Then Rosalie Pig broke the old door of her pen and the only man who could make a new one was busy digging out snowdrifts on behalf of the council. Oh, the amazing things we had to do to keep the enormous old sow under control until he could make a steel gate to allow her to wander in her own private yard once more.

Rosalie, a Gloucester Old Spot, isn't one of those pigs who needs a controlled environment. She and the others sleep warm in a good, deep straw bed and enjoy a morning constitutional, whatever the weather. But without a door on their exercise yard, they had to be fastened into their sty and the enforced house arrest didn't suit them at all. I could hear their strident cries for freedom from within, and I knew exactly how they felt. I, too, wanted out, and looked in vain for an exit.

Now, however, the new gate was fitted, and we could all breathe again. In fact, things got better in all sorts of ways. A cloud lifted. Oh, the weather was still bad – but I'd known worse. It even had its funny side. One morning an egg split open in my hand and its frozen innards plunged into a grubby snowdrift at my feet and lay there, glaring up at me from its frozen socket like a single, yellow eye.

One of my chief problems on freezing mornings has always been the provision of water for my sheep on the moor. No taps work. All troughs are frozen solid. All the other ewes lick snow. But recently a small crack appeared in the road and a positive torrent of water gushed out and steadfastly refused to freeze no matter what happened. Here I could fill my bucket. Now my sheep could drink when I folded them in at night on the piece of land that their feet and dung are reclaiming for their future use.

It's an ill wind, they say. My neighbours grumbled about that water and the roadman spent hours plotting how it could be stopped, but to me it was a sign, like a ram in the thicket.

You see, at that time I had almost decided to give up what had suddenly appeared a hopelessly unequal struggle. To give up. To go away. The prospect comforted me in a weird way. But, as I tipped the gift of water into the trough and the lucky ewes supped and swigged like my gramp when he poured his tea into his saucer, I knew different.

Old Lamb Chop used my leg to scratch an itch on her forehead, and I obliged her further with a finger nail. 'Don't worry,' I told her. 'I won't sell you all.' I looked around me at the icy wastes, then back at the trusting yellow eyes. 'Some hotter places than this will have to freeze over first!'

One of my most graphic snow-memories, though, was of an extraordinary Easter Saturday, when the dale was dislocated by a freak snowstorm, and a howling blizzard blew wet, spinning snow through every crack in every wall, soaking, freezing, burying and blinding as though someone, somewhere, had pointed it in our direction and said 'Kill!'

The day began with a panic – it was snowing hard and I thought I must have done a sort of Rip Van Winkle and lain down in April and woken up in January. Through the first early mistiness of the departure of a good night's sound sleep rang the terrible inner alarm – my sheep!

Lambing had finished but up there on that moor were the whole flock, newly turned-out, with their youngsters at foot. The lambs were growing now, fit and strong, but they were far too small to be left alone in a blizzard and they would shelter in the old gully behind the intake wall, as they did every night, not realising that the howling north-easter was filling their special, secret place, with drifting snow. How long had it been falling? Was I too late?

The wind scoured the edges of my ears and took my breath away and replaced it with stinging gravel. I toiled up the hill and along the road, burdened with as much hay as I could carry, taking a short cut across the top of the quarry to the place where I knew my sheep ought to be.

And there they were. I can find no way to tell you my joy and relief as they moved towards me, calling and shaking the snow from their backs where it had settled in large quantities. Lucky sheep, they had already shed the burden of their lambs and were much better able to face the conditions than the still-pregnant ewes further along the wall.

I counted the lambs in an agony of apprehension, but they were all there and they even played a while in the shelter of the gutter. I climbed down and lifted them all out because their little legs couldn't cope with the drifts that had piled up around them. I shiver to think now that if I hadn't gone for them, they would all have died there because by night the great gutter was filled level.

We set off with the blizzard behind us and I fastened them all in their own little intake where a group of spindly birch trees broke up the driving snow into more manageable portions.

On the way back I checked all the other sheep along the wall, getting them on to their feet and lessening their snow burden until they could be rescued. But I couldn't find Snuff, somewhere in the inside fields, and I searched and searched.

When I found her, she and Lamp Chop were almost covered in the snow that still whirled on and on. I got them on their feet, fed them and laid plans to lead them down the fields to the house and safety. Daisy May huddled with her back to the wind and Snuff's lambs, Peter and Paul, stood with their eyes tight shut, shivering. They were in a corner, between two stone walls but these were now buried in great, white pillows. The noise of the wind was frightening. The tiny flakes flew parallel to the ground and I was wet to the skin.

I returned with a bucket and stick, to bribe and coerce as necessary but neither was any use. For the first time in her long and pampered life, old Snuff was afraid, and Lamb Chop's Swaledale instincts told her to stay where she was and wait out the storm. But the narrow corner was filling in fast and I began to panic.

I got them as far as the first field but they turned back. I went home shaking with cold and frustration, returning with yet another bucket of food.

Just outside our gate I felt a pull on the bucket. Willis, the borrowed billy goat, was following me. I was angry and clouted him – that was all I needed. I selected a track through deeper snow – that'd stop him – but it didn't. I ran as fast as I could but still he followed, and, with hysteria rapidly taking control of me, I shrieked at him like a fishwife and he just looked at me with his inscrutable yellow eyes. In those eyes was a kaleidoscope of pictures – the scapegoat, following in the wilderness, the stable-goat, leading precious horses to safety from fire, and the Judas goat, leading terrified sheep on to ships in the docks. 'Willis, old man,' I said, ashamed, 'come with me.'

And he came. And it worked. In the small hours of the morning there wound down the hill a strange caravan. I led, with stick and bucket, and behind me came Willis, with two sheep and three lambs at his heels. As my old Gran used to say, 'When the Lord don't come, He sends.'

Most of the time, though, I can still summon up that within me which can enjoy snow. Last year I had a great day's sledging. On that one particular day, the snow was just right – a slight thaw the day before and a frost during the night had slicked the surface of the covering on the fields and it shimmered rock-hard in the morning sun.

Up till then, the snow had only shown its less desirable consistencies. We'd had the floundery, welly-grabbing sort; the new-fallen snow all whipped up and powdery that looks so beautiful and lies so perfect that it seems a shame to walk on it – but when you have to, it makes matters as awkward as possible by refusing to carry so much as a mouse's weight and swallowing human legs thigh-deep at every back-aching step.

That was the sort I tried to walk on early one morning as I followed a ploughed-out track across the moor in an attempt to get a change of clothes to Nancy, who was snowed-out and staying with a school friend. I had intended to give my little parcel to one of the village girls before the school bus left and ask her to give it to Nan – but that treacherous, tiring snow made me 20 minutes too late, and the village constable took it into Northallerton with him and left it at the school office. It's true what foreigners say – our policemen are wonderful, coping cheerfully with any local crises, from sheep-rustling to the providing of clean underwear for underprivileged children.

And then we had the wet and woebegone sort of snow. The kind that is merely slush on city streets, but out here in the country it's more like a failed attempt at sorbet, and it tracks in on feet, ruins carpets and makes crystalline tidemarks on your shoes. That's the stage the snow had got to by the middle of the week when I had to go to town for supplies and wore what the kids call my 'better boots' – an ancient suede pair from the Oxfam shop which I have had for years and hold in great affection.

That's the sort of snow that makes me wonder why people go off on holiday in search of the stuff.

But that morning, when I went up to feed the sheep I found the gleaming blue-white crust that crunched under my feet and realised that here, at last, was the sledging snow. Not that I was pleased to see it at first. I had dragged 15 bags of stockfeed potatoes down through the powdery stuff and 30 hundredweight of animal feed, four stone at a time on my shoulders, through the slush. Now here was good, solid sledging snow at a time when I had no real use for it. So I made one.

I got the little sledge out and pushed it in front of me, bobsleigh-style till it got a bit of a start, then leapt aboard and let go! It didn't go all that fast at first, because of the rust on the runners, and Turpin capered round and round me as I jerked and juddered down the hill – but after a time or two it was real Cresta stuff, with the wind in my face and the dog yapping at a clean pair of heels.

What a sight it must have been – but there were only a couple of rabbits to see me go sailing by – wheeee!

On one special day in the middle of winter, it was bitterly cold outside. There was a white blanket of clammy fog as though the world were under dust-sheets, waiting to have its chimney swept, and a strange sensation of still being under a ceiling even in the middle of a field.

Everything was still there, but you had to take it on trust

when you were more than a few yards away, and when I went out first thing to spread a helping of hay for the creatures who live just outside the house, it took two minutes to still the clamouring for breakfasters, and ten just to look at what had happened to the awkward oak tree and the gnarled damson which support the ends of my clothes line.

The damson is a very old lady, an untidy, twiggy, shock-headed sort of tree; the oak is a mere stripling whose growth year by year is still visible, like a human adolescent. Their trunks are far enough apart to get a week's wash strung between them, but higher up, they touch and twine and it was this entanglement of bare branches that held my attention as I stood under the clothes lines.

These branches have hooked the loops out of my towels and made holes in my tights. They have dripped sludge on white school blouses and made a safe haven for little birds which do unspeakable things on thermal vests. I have thought often that it would be a good idea to trim them up a bit. But as I looked up into them that morning and saw what the hoarfrost had done, I felt the same silent awe as a visitor staring up into the fan tracery of a cathedral roof.

The lambs' tails on the little hazel bush by the stream were hanging stiff and still like diamond earrings on a row of debutantes, waiting to curtsey to royalty, and I spared them a glance of two – but they were lovely the day before when I brushed their yellow fatness with the back of my hand and blew off the pollen like a pinch of golden snuff.

No, the real revelation was the transformation of the washing-trees, and in the very early morning, while the day was still getting into gear, I stood still and wondered at it. But not for long. The ground was so crisp and hard that I had skipped out in my slippers and my feet were freezing.

Rosalie Pig brought me back to reality with a good-morning grunt and I scuttled in to get a bucket of pignuts and to dress properly for the weather. Turpin had already fetched my wellies, and my thick socks were in the oven, on

250 deg. F. with my gloves on the bottom shelf.

Even in the kitchen my breath made clouds, and the dishcloth was frozen to the draining board. Up on the edge of the moor, the sheep were waiting. I loaded myself up with half a bale of hay and set off to let them out for a day among the heather.

It was cold outside. There'd be nipped ears and frozen noses to come, and I should have to watch out for ice on the road. I put the kettle on low for a cup of tea when I got back. But however cold it was and whether or not I measured my length on the road, I felt better for having seen, just for those few quiet moments, the transformation of the washing-trees.

It was some measure of consolation for what followed. Why did They have to wait until it was umpteen degrees below to come and put the finishing touches to our water tank? This involved turning off the water for the interminable time it took for Their special slow-setting cement to solidify. Whether They got extra points for making sure it was the Christmas holidays, with a group of Robert's friends staying with us, and thereby scoring maximum inconvenience I couldn't say, but They certainly deserved them.

The loo was the first of the water-based facilities to withdraw its support and I could only marvel at the prodigious voiding of a handful of small boys who couldn't fetch a bucket of water if Hell had them. Almost straight away the cold tap coughed up a little rusty dribble and dried up.

I issued an edict that all water must be fetched from the pond in buckets, but that was an icy prospect on a tinkling, frosty morning and, although I grumbled self-righteously each time I saw someone just filling one kettle from the hot tap, or just running a drop of warm comfort ovr tingling snow-baller's fingers, I must confess to filching a drop myself, now and then, when it was just too much trouble to get my wellies on to go outside.

This, of course, had the inevitable result. The supply in the header tank failed and without a full quota in the hot water system, we dared not light the sitting room fire. So we froze.

On the Sunday afternoon we went out, and it cheered me to remember, on and off, throughout the goat society meeting I attended, that I would be able to turn on the stoptap on my way down the hill and Mafeking would be relieved. I could hardly wait.

But wait I did, because when I turned on the tap and ran down the hill to be sure I could turn the house-taps off if they happened to have been left on, learning from my bitter experience of when we last played this game, I stood panting in the kitchen for about 20 minutes before it sank in that something had gone wrong. There was no water coming through.

At the time there was ice on the insides of the windows. There was a crust on top of the washing-up bowl and the dishcloth was all crisp and stuck to the draining board. So why it didn't occur to me that the wretched pipe, still waiting to be covered up, had frozen solid, I can't imagine. I fiddled for hours, turning taps till they came to bits in my hand and sucking and blowing at them until my face was sore. We all went to bed unwashed and cold.

The next day was even colder and I galloped up the hill to the tank with kettles of water which was boiling when I left the house and little better than lukewarm when I tipped it over the stiff black pipe. By lunchtime, though, we had water once again and a great fire roaring up the chimney.

But while I was pottering about at the tank, in total despair, Bean Goose had been pottering, too, and when I set off back down the hill he watched me almost as far as the house, then launched himself to run after me. He twinkled down on the tips of his orange toes, then he seemed to open his great wings to steady himself. He seemed every bit as surprised as I was when, with one flap and several great squawks, he rose in the air and, with much commotion, managed to keep himself aloft till he cleared the plum trees and sailed on an invisible rope down to the middle of the little pasture below the house.

I ran to him to see if he was all right and as I went I heard the children's worried voices in the yard. 'What was that?' 'It was Bean.' 'Where's he going?' 'Flying South – geese do.' 'Where's Mum off?' 'Same, I expect.' 'Can't say I blame her.' And they all trooped into the house to get the fire going.

This Great Responsibility

A speckled cat and a tame hare
Eat at my hearthstone
And sleep there;
And both look up to me alone
For learning and defence
As I look up to Providence.

I start out of my sleep to think
Some day I may forget
Their food and drink
Or, the house door left unshut,
The hare may run till it's found
The horn's sweet note and the tooth of the hound.

I hear a burden that might well try
Men that do all by rule
And what can I
That am a wandering-witted fool
But pray to God that he ease
My great responsibilities.

W. B. YEATS

It was always a source of anguish to me that I could never quite convince anyone who has not wholeheartedly entered into the life of a hill farmer, that it is possible to fill one's time, one's thoughts, every waking moment of one's day and the sudden, wide-awake moments of the occasional troubled night with plans, worries and fears that are totally concerned with livestock. I found it came easily.

I resented the edge of irritation in the voices of friends who felt slighted when I thrust my commitment under their noses; I found it hard not to rise to the hint of a sneer from members of my family who could not, or, as I preferred to see it, would not – understand the seriousness with which I took these self-imposed disciplines of milking, feeding, seeking, finding and belonging.

I could not explain, even to myself, that I had developed them to the point where they were ends in themselves, satisfying and fulfilling needs I dared not acknowledge, blinding me to so much that I would rather not see. Now and again, though, something would happen to me, through me, because or in spite of me, that gave me a clue as to my status among it all. And I could evaluate or ignore it as I chose.

Once upon a time there was a family of rather varied individuals who lived in a red-brick house with bay windows. I don't really remember them all that well, but I know they had two brown spaniels and a black cat with kittens, white wooden chairs and a green telephone. This last resides in my box of 'mother's treasures' and is a source of wonder to the children who can't imagine their mother ever having a use for a tiny lead telephone no bigger than a fingernail.

But I did, for the telephone served the family who lived in the dolls' house my father made for me when I was small. It was a perfect model of my grandmother's house, and as I watched Nancy and her friends refurbishing it for the modern, skinny, big-bosomed dolls that looked so out of place sprawled on the utility furniture, I remembered very clearly what it was like to have such absolute power over the comings and goings of these little captives whose eyes, had they been able to see with them, would have had trouble conveying to their little match-head brains the vastness of me; the brains in turn would scarcely have conceived of my omnipotence.

I enjoyed my dolls' house, granted, but I was always a little afraid of it, and of the responsibility implied in the closing of the hinged walls on whatever situation I had decreed should be.

I was thinking about that as I fished Ferret out of the pond. A few weeks earlier, one of our less intelligent ducks was presiding over a clutch of hatching eggs in a nest on top of an ant hill. It is a measure of her stupidity that she nested in such a situation a second time, after having been shown the year before that an ant hill is a bad place to sit for a month. Not that the ants bit her, they didn't. I hardly ever saw one crawl over her, but they objected so strongly to her presence that they moved their nest to the other side of the wall – taking with them every whisker of the precious down with which she had lined hers. Exactly the same thing happened this time, resulting in a hard, deep nest in which the eggs were far more at risk than would have been necessary had she nested in a more normal place. It was therefore unavoidable that she should smash at least one egg in the turning and trampling of her hopeful sit-in, and that smashed egg became Ferret.

It was after she had left the nest with what ducklings she had hatched successfully that I checked the empty nest to see what casualties were left, two dead ducklings and a smashed egg, from whose ruptured inner membrane a thin trickle of blood flowed. I held out little hope, even though the pulsating of the sad and sticky soul within showed me that there was still life, of a sort. I pulled aside the thick, white skin, and saw clearly that the great swollen yolk-sac on which the unhatched chick feeds was still far too much in evidence for the duckling to be mature. I carried the whole unpleasant mess and gave it to a broody hen, Snow White, only a yearling herself and a little bewildered by the fact that the eggs she was hatching were being systematically pinched one by one by Rose Red, another pullet from the same brood, who had opted to nest right alongside.

A noisy, aggressive bird, Rose Red would work her beak under poor Snow White's feathers and scoop out her eggs, tucking them fussily under her own russet bosom. Placid little Snow White would wait until Rose Red got off her nest to feed, and then quietly filch them all back again. They never left the nests simultaneously and I feared that the eggs would never have a chance to cool off. All the same, they had begun to hatch when I offered Snow White this poor destroyed duck, just to see if her gentle, fussing care would do the trick. It did. Then, just as he poked his head for the first time from under her soft, white wing, Rose Red, clucking menacingly, swooped on him and stuffed him, with the other hatchlings, beneath her, leaving Snow White with all the eggs. It seemed so unfair that I took Snow White, along with all the living chicks and put her in a coop with a run, determined that Rose Red should hatch the rest herself, and that they should share the fulfilment of motherhood as seemed more fitting to my selfish view. I didn't stop to think that they might have had some mutual arrangement beyond my arrogant understanding. Within 24 hours I regretted my interference.

Rose Red never returned to her nest. For three weeks she sat, noisily angry, on the top of the run where Snow White, sweet and placid as ever, tended the chicks. The little duckling grew and flourished. I christened him Ferret, because that's what he looked like peeping from his feathered stronghold. Still Rose Red fumed and swore on the top of the run.

At last I let them out, thinking that Rose Red would surely by now be cured of her frustration. Not a bit of it. She plopped down beside the scurrying chicks, began clucking expertly, and called about half of them to her. Snow White bobbed her head in deference and together they led their shared family to the likeliest scratching-grounds.

I saw them cope with a threat from the cat in perfect co-ordination. Rose Red flew at him while Snow White called the babies under her opened wings. At about three o'clock there came a terrible commotion. I looked out of the window to see Rose Red in what I assumed to be a furious rage. When she kept up the performance for longer than I felt I could tolerate, I went out to see what was upsetting her so much. It was Ferret. He had gone to the pond to drink and fallen in, or maybe even walked in, with his instinct taking him where it should have been safe for him to go. His soft white down, devoid of the yellow grease his real mother had imparted to his siblings, was sodden and clinging to him like rat-fur. A few moments longer and he would have drowned. I fished him out and set him on his unlikely little legs. Rose Red clucked him to follow and led him back to where Snow White was waiting to warm him fondly until he was feeling better; she left him there and took a handful of the more active chicks on a foraging expedition.

Some things are wiser and more wonderful than we, with our supposedly superior intelligence, ever give them credit for, and I fell to wondering about the dolls' house family.

Why is it that things lie around our house as untidy nuisances until such time as there arises a use for them, when they melt away out of human ken and cannot be found?

For years we have had a length of flex with a bulb-holder on one end and a two-pin plug on the other. It was originally a thing for making lamps out of wine bottles. It has been part of our immediate environment for years and yet when I needed it desperately, a concerted hunt failed to produce a single clue as to its whereabouts.

I needed a light in the barn. Snuff was going to lamb before dawn and I had exhausted my torch batteries with nightly trailings to check her progress. I have a paraffin lamp, but that was serving as the only source of heat for

Rosalie's newborn pigs, so it couldn't be spared.

I ended up with a candle in my steadiest candlestick set up safe behind a hurdle where it couldn't be knocked over and I settled down to wait for the lamb to come. This vigil seemed at the time the least I could do for this, our oldest family retainer.

Time after time Snuff had carried twins only to miscarry one before the birth of the other, but each year she had come nearer to making the double. The previous year the dead lamb arrived after his living sister, Snufkin, but he was wrapped in a heavy caul and even had he been living, he would not have lasted long without some human help in escaping his leathery prison.

This time, if there was the slightest chance of two lambs surviving, I wanted to be there in time to take it, so I settled down and waited. The candle threw soft shadows on the hewn stones and only the old ewe's heavy breathing stirred the silence. It was as if the whole world were holding its breath with me, waiting for the precious gift of a new life.

I had done my best to give Snuff the privacy to which she was entitled. Snufkin and the goats slept outside the closed door and I had hidden in a heap of straw up in the granary that overlooked my lambing pen. I watched and listened.

And at last it was there, shaking its heavy head and steaming gently as the natal slime evaporated from the warm and perfect body and Snuff started the age-old guttural murmuring as she cleaned her little one. It looked a fine big lamb. I hauled myself nearer to the edge of the granary. In a matter of minutes Snuff lay down again and strained hard with her feet against the bottom of the wall.

Another head appeared. And a foot. Only one foot.

I slipped quietly down beside her and looked carefully. This one was, apparently, as big as the first. Its sac was broken and it sneezed. My joy threatened to choke me as I took the one leg gently in my hand, wondering whether to try to bring its shoulders through despite the trailing leg or to reach for the missing foot. Snuff decided. With a final effort she pushed it into the world just as it was and spun round to welcome it with her caressing tongue. I drew back into the shadows and sat down.

The joy hurt, but I hugged it to me like a secret pain and waited, savouring every moment until both lambs were on their feet. Only then did I take each lamb gently and spray the navel cords with terramycin, just in case. Science has its place, alongside nature. The lambs were both gimmers.

Then, abruptly, Snuff left the twins and turned her back on them. She thrust her feet against the bottom of the wall, flung her head up, and pushed once more with all her might.

And slowly, unbelievably, there came forth two more feet, one more blunt noughts-and-crosses nose, and a third long, strong body. The sac was unbroken so I tore it to release the damp little face, wiped the slime from the mouth and then withdrew to my corner as Snuff turned to greet her third live lamb, which spluttered crossly and staggered to its feet. It, too, was a gimmer.

The old sheep was delighted. She busied herself with the babies, wheeling and turning until she threatened to tread on one in her anxiety to be scrupulously fair with her mothering. Having reared twins myself, I appreciated the problem. I carried all three lambs a foot or two to a clean dry place and helped ensure that each one had her fair share of the colostrum – the first, precious milk that nature sends to clear the dark, sticky meconium from the internal works of newborn creatures and to impart to the young ones a share of the disease antibodies built up by their mother.

Here again, science was aiding nature. I had injected Snuff a fortnight earlier with a booster dose of vaccine against the worst threats her babies would encounter during their first few weeks, and as they fumbled and spluttered they were, through the colostrum, protecting themselves even more than Nature could have arranged.

I lay in the straw and Snuff lay beside me, while the babies explored their world, which consisted, for the time being, of a small portion of the old stone barn. Outside, the wind howled and snowflakes whirled, looking for crannies to creep in upon us. Outside Snufkin cried. Tomorrow she would meet her sisters, but for now they were only Snuff's, and mine. The candle threw its gentle glow and everything dithered between bright gold and purplish-black in the shifting, liquid light, and the lambs pottered, big-shadowed, on stiff little legs, thrusting and bumping against my face in their search for food and comfort.

It was only when I stood up at last to go back home to bed I realised how tired I was. Nancy had stayed up and made a cup of tea. 'Has she had it?' I took her out again and showed her, for I couldn't bear simply to tell her and send her off to bed. 'Milly – Molly – Mandy?' I asked, and she nodded, too happy to speak.

Lambing time, though, is always a period of great soul-searching as the self-imposed responsibility reaches its great spring-time peak. It went well that year, I recall.

Quite early in the proceedings little June gave birth to two lambs, which tried to scuttle after her as she pottered round the field. April, we called the first one, and the second, not May – we'd already had a May – but Daisy May. All the others produced fine, big single lambs, all without much trouble, and only one of the first-timers needed any help in sorting out at which end her son needed to suck.

I waited patiently for Lamb Chop. Now Lamb Chop, as those who have come to know the flock will remember, doesn't like newborn lambs, especially her own. She can't bring herself to lick or mother the nasty, wet things. Year after year she has waited. In wet weather I have stepped in and penned her, showing her as patiently as if she were just a shearling what she must do. In dry weather I have waited, my heart going out to the filthy little creature that wailed its way from one ewe to another, getting butted for its pains, until Lamb Chop finally decided to accept it, ending up as she had always done, the best and most devoted of mothers.

June's babies grew, but not a lot, flourished, but not exceptionally and at last began to fade a little at a time, as her small body failed to take up the challenge of twins and she achieved her maximum milk yield which was obviously just not going to be enough. Sadly I took Daisy May home and began to feed her with goat milk, along with the two young goats and the two little piglets already in my spring nursery.

Before long she would skip up to me and take her bottle like an old hand and I rediscovered the pleasure of a warm, wriggling lamb thrusting its blunt face against mine in pure cupboard love.

Lamb Chop's time came and she waddled about and fussed as she always does. Hour after hour with nothing to show. Just thinking about it, not really working, staring into space. Night came. All the books say that, even if a ewe is in trouble a shepherd has hours to spare. Don't rush things, they tell you. Give Nature time, they say.

But I was worried and played with the alarm clock, setting it two hours ahead each time I lay down for a bit of sleep. Ten, twelve, two, four, up, dress, and paddle like a zombie to the field, torch in hand. No sign. No progress. No little feet to be seen, no obvious signs of struggle.

But somewhere between four and six she lambed.

I saw her sitting there on the crest of the hill with a lamb beside her. I ran. She got up and called to me, but didn't look at the lamb. A posterior presentation, I could clearly see; the sac still wrapped round its head, lying in an attitude of utter peace, and quite dead.

'You were supposed to lick it,' I said dully. 'You what?' she seemed to say.

June came to peer at the dead body so I picked it up and hurled it out of sight, I would bury it later. Little April ducked and ran. And then I thought of Daisy May. It just might not be too late. I took Lamb Chop down to the house and fetched my precious pet lamb.

Now Daisy May took to Lamb Chop straight away but I had to hold the old girl while she suckled. I had often done the same, though, for her own lambs. I persevered, and so did Daisy May, following her new mother but never pressing, never insisting.

And by the end of the very first day, it was right. The old magic worked as Lamb Chop's delayed reaction happened yet again and she licked and muttered as Daisy May sucked and sucked and twirled her woolly tail. Although she was two weeks old she played the newborn nursling perfectly and I watched in delight as the old picture came to life once more. And just once, Daisy May peeped out from below Lamb Chop's huge fleece with a knowing look for her old foster-mother. Just once.

Two years passed, and lambing time came again with the inevitability that brings its own strange comfort. One of the things about country life that is often hard to explain to people not acquainted with its mysteries is the nature of its repetitiveness; the way it rolls along on a twelve-month cycle of total predictability. Round and round it all goes in a sort of spiral, a continuous line, progressing forwards just a little at each spin, so that even though the seasons come and go with the utter certainty of all foregone conclusions, it never actually covers the same ground twice.

Now there's a bit of rural philosphy for you! You'll have to forgive me, though, because this is the time of year when anyone who is remotely connected with sheep or shepherding develops a tendency to become a bit whimsical. It's caused by the disrupted sleep-patterns and unsocial hours of lambing time.

And as it happens, I did get a little shiver of déja-vu when I went for my mid-morning check and saw what Daisy May was licking solicitously in the hazy sunshine. From the far end of the field I could see the lamb lying at her feet. And I knew it was dead. There is nothing quite like the anguish of knowing, long before a sheep has guessed at it, that her lamb is dead. I could see the soft and silly creature, licking and loving, working so hard to get her baby to stand and suck, and I could see the outstretched hind legs, the fast-asleep attitude, of a lamb that has come into the world back-feet-first, and has drowned on the way.

And then the if-only's begin. If only I'd been there ten minutes sooner. If only I'd had some land nearer the house. If only the ewe had lambed quicker, cutting down the time between the snapping of the navel cord and the first vital gulp of air. If only . . . if only. But it was no good. The damage to the poor little creature was irreparable. Oh, I tried – I inflated the tiny lungs carefully, but the sloshing of the liquid inside them was deafening. I took the hind legs and whirled it round my head – a desperate measure, but I've known it succeed. But this time it wasn't going to work.

And so I contacted a friend's lamb-bank, and within a couple of hours was listening to another sad story.

Precious, the Masham lamb, had also been born during the night. Her twin had died, and only an hour or so under an infra-red lamp had saved Precious herself. Her mother had mastitis. Precious needed a foster-mother. I asked my friend to bring her to me. I had brought Daisy May and her dead baby down to the house, and as I listened to Precious's story, I gently removed the soft, warm skin from the limp body. Not the nicest of jobs, but it was done with love, and with the best of motives. I slipped the skin onto Precious, with her legs threaded carefully through the holes left by the legs of the former occupant. I threaded her tail through the last hole, fixed it all underneath with two safety pins, and took the little parcel out to Daisy May, who was howling for the baby she'd seen me take away.

'Here, you daft thing – I've mended it for you . . .,' and she was so busy licking and fussing at this, 'her' lamb, that she didn't even look up to thank me. But the next day, when I went up to the field to feed the sheep, Daisy May was in the front of the queue and her child galloped behind her, both taking for granted their devotion to each other, and quite ignorant of my part in the proceedings.

There is nothing, too, quite like the pleasure of having got it right, and I watched them for a long time before I turned and went home to start the waiting for the next ewe to lamb.

And only then did the two years slip away, and I saw the irony of what had happened and my own place in it all. How easy it would have been to lie – to re-cast the drama so that it all fell pat, just like this – and now that fate had done it for me, I felt a little cheated.

In a letter wherein this third book was proposed my publishers' editor suggested I 'followed the vicissitudes of your suckling lambs from birth till the births of lambs of their own'.

The thought did not appeal to me at the time. I felt it was perhaps a little trite! I am always somewhat wary of the animal anecdote that slips too easily into the slot assigned to it.

When I first began to take Turpin among the sheep, I did not attempt any fancy training. All I asked was that he should observe the routine I had established and seek only to oil the wheels a little when requested. Otherwise he was expected merely to attend in an advisory capacity.

I used to let him drive the sheep out on to the moor on winter mornings. Now and again, though, some little thing would happen to upset the routine, and all hell broke loose. One morning, one of the sheep had crept through a hole into a small plantation that adjoins their field. Turpin whisked all the others out in fine style, feeling he'd done a good job – although the old dears would have gone out anyway, as they'd been trained for far longer than he had.

Then it took a further quarter of an hour to get one daft sheep out of one small hole, back into the field and out to the moor with the rest, who had, by this time, finished their food and were all trying to get back in again to see what they were missing. On top of that, several 'foreign' sheep had come to clear up anything ours might have left, and when I tried to send these back to whence they had come, Turpin gathered up a few of ours as well, and was so excited I couldn't prevail upon him to calm down and put matters right. It was a sort of half-organised chaos and I did a lot of shouting. Bloody dog; bloody, bloody sheep, etcetera.

But when it was all over, and matters had been brought to a successful conclusion, I remembered a line of Gavin Maxwell's that has been of much comfort, to the effect that if animals do not occasionally allow liberty to instinct, they will in time shed the rest of their positive qualities as well, and be left with nothing but charm. Heaven forbid!

The heaviest responsibilies, though, are always those undertaken for the first time, or under scrutiny. Or both.

When I had sold Magnus, and crashed the motorbike, I used the insurance money to buy a Jersey heifer. The reasoning was simple. The biggest money-spinners on the farm were the pigs. They were also the greatest expense. I was already doing all I could to ensure their maximum productivity. Thus the only way I could increase their profit-margin was to cut down on the overheads. A supply of high butter-fat milk would turn quickly to cash when fed to pigs. Oh, what a businesswoman I had become!

It was a long-term plan, of course. In order to ensure that milk-supply, I had to arrange a mating, ensure a pregnancy and choreograph a calving. I had it all worked out long before the lovely creature reached her adolescence.

But one Sunday the whole thing collapsed around my ears.

Up until that Sunday, I had enjoyed the radio serial *The King must Die*. That week, though, as I settled down in bed to listen to the latest episode, I couldn't keep my mind on the story. Not, that is, until the part where the Cretans arrived bringing Theseus a great, white bull, which he accepted in spite of the mystic warning 'Loose not the bull from the sea'. Needless-to-say, the bull was loosed, and to Theseus, experienced in the Cretan bull-courts, fell the task of taming the great beast and leading it back to the city. Great stuff. I was all ears as soon as he mentioned that he wanted a sweet little heifer with which to entice the mighty monster into his net. I could have told him all about that. By that evening I had just about had my fill of big white bulls and innocent little heifers.

When Charity came into season, which she had done every three weeks since she was ten months old, she left nobody in any doubt that there was something lacking in her little world. She bawled and bellowed, thoroughly upsetting all the cattle within earshot, and became playful and silly, tossing her head and kicking her heels and attempting to mount anything that stood still long enough for her to try it.

Most of the time she was the sweetest, most biddable little Jersey heifer that ever graced a pasture. People would stop their cars to take pictures of her, especially when she wore the floppy straw hat that protected her from the sun when she was tethered at the roadside. She had the makings of the archetypal cow, all level honest eyes and imperturbable disposition.

But every three weeks she became a positive fiend, attacking the clothes on the line if I kept her in the yard, and creating a public nuisance with her hoydenish behaviour if she was left in the field with the lambs.

On the Saturday morning, two game old ladies had set off along the footpath from Jim's farm to ours, but didn't get far before they returned, vowing to find another route. 'The bull,' they said 'was acting strangely.' There was no bull along that footpath, just Charity, in one of her silly moods.

On Saturday night she was still there. On Sunday morning she had gone. I searched along the wide green footpath where she had been confined for safety from Jim's Limousin bull, and found that someone – perhaps the fleeing ladies –

had left open the gate at the far end of the path, and my beloved little heifer could have been, in theory, anywhere in the maze of green fields that lay below. But I knew with a sinking heart just where she'd be. Jim and his wife came to help me search but I set off, with a piece of borrowed rope, across the river and up the other side of the valley to where more distant neighbours kept a huge suckler herd, attended by a vast Charolais. She grazed in happy companionship with a group of the creamy-white calves with the big heads and massive shoulders of their father, who was nowhere to be seen. He had taken his pleasure and gone. I tied the rope to Charity's collar, and she trotted with me like a well-behaved dog until we came back to the river, where Jim helped me to get her back onto his territory and together we all set off for mine. But what to do now?

The best laid plans of mice and men gang aft aglae, but those of stock farmers are even less to be depended upon. I asked advice and was regaled in turn with stories of heifers who had to be slaughtered when they could not deliver big continental calves and stories of great struggles that ended in varying degrees of disaster. And there were the tales, too, of heifers much smaller than Charity who survived, reared their calves, and went on to become, always 'the best cow in the herd'. I went to see the bull's owners, and they rewarded me with more stories in about equal quantities. All that worried me was that I should do the best for Charity. At fourteen months she was surely too young, but none of my neighbours would commit themselves as to what they would do if they were me, here, now.

I decided to phone the vet first thing on Monday morning, and ask his advice. And I lay in bed listening to the serial, but with only half a heart.

We decided on an abortion. An injection from the vet, a slight, anonymous discharge and a month later her reproductive cycle began again and she became once more a responsibility to me and a threat to old ladies. Towards the end of the summer, I decided that it was time. I had already got Jim's permission to use his Limousin bull, and as Charity called desperately from the yard, I set off to fetch him from the fields around the house.

He didn't seem particularly keen. Across the river, the Charolais proclaimed his willingness to oblige, but the Limousin lay under the oak tree, sound asleep. I prodded him with a stick. He sighed, but that was all. In the end I tied a rope to Charity's collar and walked her past the bull once or twice. He rose slowly to his feet, curled his top lip in ecstatic anticipation and followed her back into the yard.

It was very early in the morning. I was anxious to supervise this encounter myself before anyone else was about. The bull was very large, the heifer rather small, and her knees were inclined to buckle before he could achieve what was necessary. The only reading I had done that threw any light on this problem was a novel by Zola, but it helped.

At Christmas the vet examined Charity and pronounced her in-calf.

Within two days of Charity's arrival, I was sitting in the barn beside the house, wondering just what I had taken on. A solemn, tawny calf, all doe-eyes and spindle-legs faced me across a bucket out of which I was trying to persuade her to drink the goat milk that was to become her staple diet. She said she would rather die. My knees ached, my arms were throbbing with the effort of forcing the innocent flower-face into the froth, and my skin crawled where the milk was drying solid on every exposed inch of it. I despaired of ever rearing her.

And now here she was two years later, a cow at last. Our Charity, who, all those months ago, seemed destined to starve to death on hunger-strike, now had a calf of her own. This was what I'd been waiting for, longing for, looking foward to – yet here I was again, knees stiff, arms aching and face and fingers itching with congealed custard desperate to get just a little of Charity's milk into her precious, perfect, beautiful, bloody-minded daughter, who said she would rather die.

And at one point, it rather looked as though she might.

For two weeks I'd been watching Charity, peeping round corners and spying like a thing possessed. Almost all the neighbours asked after her at every opportunity. Offers of help should she have difficulty came from the most unexpected quarters, but when she finally calved it was all so quick and so easy that the damp ginger heifer seemed almost too easily won to be true. I cleared a little mucus from her mouth and nostrils, and left Charity to do the rest. She was clearly in control of the situation, and her love and concern for her new baby were endearingly obvious.

The baby's breathing seemed a bit rattly, but I thought no more about it. I carefully applied the big yellow eartag I'd been given by Jim when I told him I'd borrowed his bull. My own personal herd number, allocated by the Ministry of Agriculture, and a big, proud number '1'.

But seven hours later, the calf still hadn't suckled. Her breathing was loud and harsh. She could be persuaded to stand, but the effort made her gasp and wheeze. I telephoned the vet.

A course of injections, he said, would clear matters up. She had inhaled a little fluid during her birth. I must try to get a drop of milk into her before night. So that was how I came to be crouched in the straw, the defiant calf stretched across my knees, her head twisted as far as possible away from where I wanted it to be. It was clearly hopeless to expect her to suck. I was too tired to lift her any more and experience had convinced me that there is no limit to the length of time a really determined calf can hold a cow's teat in its mouth without sucking – like the forbearance associated with the chewing of fruit gums . . .

So we lay there, under the patient little cow. My left hand held the calf's muzzle, the first two fingers thrust into her mouth to keep it open. My right reached wearily up to grasp the teat, squeezing gently at intervals so that a jet of golden colostrum was directed into the calf's mouth. Or up her nose. Or down my neck. Or up my arm.

But it worked. I was late to bed, and late up in the morning. The sun shone bright and warm on the new baby, whose breathing was now nearly normal. I realised she hadn't even got a name. What would suit her? Something French, in honour of her father. Something that expressed all the pride and love that still glowed on the face of the little cow. Something that reflected all the hope and the waiting. A special name for someone greatly longed-for – Désirée.

The school holidays were over. We got right to the last week before cash-flow problems caused a temporary breakdown of communications with the village grocer, which isn't bad – usually anorexia impecuniosa (failure to eat through lack of ready money) sets in about half-way through. For those of us whose kids are entitled to free school meals in term time, it's a struggle to feed them during the holidays. I'd turned my hand to all sorts of things in the previous six weeks – stacking hay, stacking straw, shovelling barley, building walls and stapling up what seemed like a hundred miles of barbed wire.

At the penultimate weekend, I went to help a neighbour to bag some silage. Now, silage is something I'd never had a lot to do with at close quarters; it's only just becoming popular up here in the hills as an alternative to hay. Instead of being dried to make hay, the cut grass is 'ensiled' – stored in such a way that air is excluded from it – and is dug out in winter in great lumps smelling of rough cider if it's been made properly, and rotten grass-mowings if it hasn't. One of the ways of doing this is to make the cut grass into big round bales and put them into skintight polythene bags to wait till winter. It is a process much easier described than carried out, but even so I could not find a turn of phrase in keeping with my image as a gentlewoman, so you must use your imagination!

And on the following Monday, for the sake of the common good and the village grocer, I sold Désirée. We knew all along we couldn't keep our lovely calf beyond the beginning of winter, and I had dreaded parting with her, so when George-next-door asked if I would sell her to be reared by a cow of his that had lost her own calf, I agreed after much soul-searching. The thing that made up my mind was the fact that George intends keeping her as a replacement heifer for his own herd. None of the usual misgivings about the humane-killer and the butcher's knife. It would be almost as good as keeping her ourselves, I told myself, and everyone else.

For part of the responsibility – the heavier part, as time goes on – is the justifying of such decisions to the many people who have come, through my writing, to share in the farm and its inhabitants. It feels sometimes as if I have begun to carry the additional burden of other people's dreams, and I am afraid of betraying them, of being caught out in conduct unbecoming to the image they have of me. And there we have the whole sad paradox. In order to rationalise my chosen existence, to explain it to others and to myself, I must either trivialise it into some rural fairytale, or elevate it to epic proportions quite unsuited to the basic ingredients. And I must cast myself – but as whom? – St Francis or Dr Moreau? And therein lies a yet greater responsibility.

On the Tuesday, I went on to George's farm to help him and his father, Jim, with the annual brucellosis test. For a woman not born to withstand Yorkshire ways, that takes courage. Anyone who has ever read James Herriot will have a clear picture of the goings-on on such occasions. The suckler cow on a hill farm is handled so rarely that to get near her at all is something of a challenge, and to hold her still for long enough to obtain a sample of blood from the vein in her tail she has to be driven along a narrow corridor and trapped by the head in a cunningly constructed gate.

What Herriot does not describe, however, is the scene at such a farm *before* the arrival of the veterinary surgeon. With the test scheduled for nine, there we were at five to, with George and Jim laying about the poor beasts with bits of plastic pipe and knobby boots, and the air ringing with mooing and effing and blinding, and all of it directed, seemingly, at me.

After the vet's car had drawn up, though, tempers and language mended magically. I thought wryly that the earlier scene was best looked upon as some kind of reward for my insistence on being accepted as 'one of the lads', and I decided to take it as a compliment. All the same, I made much use of the session of sweet silent thought afforded by the relatively ladylike job of booking-down the cattle as they filed past for their test. Soon Désirée would be part of all this. For a while, I quite forgot the three hundred and sixty-four days of quiet wandering over the rough pastures and saw only the poor, puzzled creatures, wild-eyed and woebegone, using their anal sphincters like noxious water-pistols as their sole defence against man's inhumanity to beast, and I wondered whether Désirée might not have come nearer to Nirvana in a tin of stewed steak.

Epilogue

As a child, in a dusty London classroom, I always enjoyed poetry lessons. Perhaps the incongruity of the environment heightened the magic, but in those days even the corniest of classroom classics drew my imagination out through the window, to Westminster Bridge or to Kew (in Lilac Time) or wherever the poet chose to send me.

I spent a great deal of time in those days with Yeats in the Lake Isle of Innisfree, carried along by the simple lines extolling the basic existence in a rural environment, long before such easy jargon entered my vocabulary. It was all part of the dream I was building for myself and I could see clearly the small cabin in the bee-loud glade and on summer evenings I hoed imaginary beans.

Now and again I am surprised into taking stock of the situation in which I find myself – or lose myself, according to your point of view – and fall to reflecting how often it is that when dreams come true we sometimes miss the chance of celebrating just because we don't realise it has happened until we have begun to take it for granted.

Sometime ago, for instance, there was a day on which it rained as though it had just found out how, and I went out armed with a few cc's of Penicillin in a hypodermic to attack a couple of lambs with joint ill. They belonged to old Henry and his wife, who had come to depend on my help. This was to be the last in their course of injections and to miss it should have been both unforgivable and expensive, but oh how it rained as I searched the miserable dripping flock for the two with red crosses on their bottoms, and the tops of my wellingtons cut unmercifully into my shins as I paddled hopelessly up and down the soggy fields until I located the outpatients under a thornbush and administered the dose, gripping soaking bodies between my knees while rain rippled along my vertebrae like a beck over pebbles.

But this was, after all, what I had longed for when I arrived. To be trusted with livestock by people who had devoted their lives to knowing what was best for them, and the pride made me limp less noticeably as I passed Henry's house on the way back home.

A more amusing example occurred a few days later, when I was cutting peat by myself up on the moor. I straightened up, albeit with difficulty, from hacking out a barrowful from the bottom row, and when I had got them transported to the drying area and spread out to dry, I decided that they had been the last for that day and gave myself permission to clock off. I strolled up as far as the Ruckle, a tall heap of stones on top of the moor, and sat down to watch the evening develop.

A couple of about my own age had got there before me, and they greeted me cheerfully; they were on a walking holiday from the Midlands and they had covered many miles that were now familiar to me in their exploration of the dale.

I told them that I had lived for a while in Birmingham, and that I was 21 years a Londoner, and, when they expressed envy at the remote loveliness of my chosen home, I warmed to them, as I was tired of defending myself against people who found it hard to imagine anyone wishing to make so dramatic a change in life-style.

They confided in me their dream. They longed to own a house somewhere like this and they began to tell me of a farm they had passed on their way up the moor. I, in the manner of listening locals, tried to place the description they gave. Sure enough, it sounded idyllic. There was a lamb, they said, so tame they had to take it back into the yard when it followed them.

I assumed it was one of my neighbours' pets. There's none so blind, they say – but the black and white sheepdog with no tail sounded familiar and the little Jersey cow. The duck sitting on her nest by the roadside, with the drake proudly on guard located it for me exactly. It was my own home they were describing, and not as the ramshackle damp-trap I had come to accept as others' vision of it, but as an embodiment of a personal dream. That's what I meant about taking things for granted.

On the other hand, though, it often proves difficult, on a day-to-day level, to keep everything in step with the general idea. I had always dreamed of a country future of peace and self-sufficiency. But that evening when I went outside to see what the children were doing I found the younger lad proving to his sister that it is possible to do wheelies on a rocking-horse, and the elder one holding a kitten to each ear to hear them purr in stereo. None of them had noticed the little goat moving methodically along the cherished bean rows. However, at that time it was still not too late to replant them.

In the epilogue to my first book, which kind readers have told me they found moving, I mentioned the advent in the dale of the first of the flat-eight bale-handling devices. 'How long, I wonder,' – I wrote – 'before one of them moves in next door?' This year, one did.

The system appears hideously complicated, with many spikes, springs and moving parts. There are two separate modules, as it were – the first takes the form of a sledge that trails behind the baler, and as each bale pops out, it drops into this thing and is sorted, shuffled and fiddled until the sledge contains eight bales in a tidy, oblong shape, like a simple kiddies' puzzle. Then a trapdoor opens and leaves the 'flat eight' sitting there, waiting for something to happen.

The second module brings about that happening. This is an oblong grab with great shark-teeth, operated by the hydraulics of a tractor. It thuds down on top of the eight-bale puzzle, digs in its steel dentures, then, at the flick of a lever, it whisks them up into the air. The tractor hurries off to wherever the bales are wanted, then the hydraulic lever persuades the device to let go again, and eight bales end up exactly where they're supposed to be.

That's it in theory. But Jim and George, who'd invested in these things for leading straw, found it wasn't all that easy, and much bad language was used in the course of the annual marathon, the bringing home of the winter's quota.

Straw, you see, is a vital part of the hill farmer's scheme of things. He uses it for fodder and for bedding, but few hill farmers grow enough cereal crops of their own to provide the quantity of straw necessary for the health and comfort of their in-wintered stock. So they buy it from the arable farmers nearer sea level, and take their own equipment down to the other farms, and bale the straw and lead it away, while the arable farmers are pawing the ground, waiting for them to clear the fields so that they can get their next cash crop underway.

It's a hectic time of year; it's also the explanation of those huge, wobbling trailers piled high with golden straw that always seem to be in front of motorists in a hurry in these parts.

So twice a day they come growling down Merton Bank, Jim, George and the two blue tractors, the latter growling because of the effort of holding back 200 bales of straw on a one-in-five, and the other two growling because the flat-eight system wasn't quite as foolproof as they'd hoped. For one thing, you see, straw doesn't weigh as much, by volume, as does hay, so the dear little bales that trickled out of the baler with the nonchalance of an old cow distributing her manurial largesse over the pastures, weren't heavy enough to trigger the mechanism in the sledge, and Jim had to come back for the special straw-wedges for the baler. I laughed a bit.

Mind you, I laughed on the other side of my face when the loads came back, and the straw had to be stored in the dutch barns, and in great stacks in the yards.

This is still a job for the casual labourer. I scaled the loaded trailer with a will, climbing the last rope just before it was removed and standing like Columbus, looking out over the New World till somebody gave the word to start chucking-off.

That was when I discovered that the bales really did weigh twice as much as last year. I refused to be bested by a mere machine, and carried on as though nothing were any different. I flexed muscles that bulged like knots in thread and pushed to the back of my mind the possibility that there might be another reason for the extra effort I was having to put in.

I have watched year by year the changes that have taken place, not only in the hill-farming scene itself, but in the cast of characters whose fortunes and faces have taken up so much of my time, of my life.

Sandra has changed from a giddy miniskirted girl to a middle-aged woman, slack-jawed and mean of mouth, with eyes like currants in an uncooked teacake, pressed in with a child's grubby fingers. George's golden hair has faded to sparse straw and his young brother who long ago tested my vows of celibacy with a consummate skill that surprised me, now has a wife and a child, and a preoccupied look.

I was so sure that we had an understanding, the Almighty and I; none of this was going to happen to me.

The intimations of mortality are bought home to us through official channels: the organ transplant donor card enclosed with the provisional driving licence; the letter accompanying the Decree Absolute, saying I am no longer eligible for a pension.

There's no halting progress, I suppose. I heard recently that the Americans have developed a new swing-wing aircraft. The wings swing forward, improving the aerodynamics. A spokesman said it is a breakthrough; I suppose it is. After all, we've got used to swing-wing aircraft whose wings swing backwards. All we need now is one whose wings swing up. And down. And up and down . . . and I smiled to myself as I watched the swallows on the telephone wire, getting in trim for the long haul to Africa.

Another poem from my school-days sang in my head.

> Allie, call the birds in,
> The birds from the sky . . .

And I saw the reason for the growing discontent. Progress has more than one face; I too had been seduced by it. One sow had become a pig-unit, the few special sheep had become a flock. In the urge to justify myself before the farmers I had sacrificed my credibility as a caring peasant. The things I wept for, the things I believed I had lost, I had thrown away by degrees. I had almost become a farmer when what I was really seeking was the old Celtic rusticity, and somehow I had lost sight of it.

I was conscious at first only of a sad sense of loss which grew harder to bear as experiment turned first to enterprise and then to success. I had wept for the dream which seemed to have betrayed me in the most cruel way there is – by coming true. Now, though, I could see where the betrayal lay.

> Allie, call the beasts in,
> The beasts, every one
> Allie calls, Allie sings,
> In they all run
> First there came
> Two black lambs
> Then a grunting Berkshire sow,

> Then a dog without a tail
> Then a red and white cow.

All the ingredients were there, but I had thrown away the element of nursery rhyme, and with it the heart of the dream.

And I smiled to myself as I recalled something else I had once written down. 'The greatest challenge of the future will be to remain true to our beginnings.'

Whether I can ever find them again remains to be seen.